B.Ball
Albany 2000

The Ultimate GOD

The Epistles of John

Jonathan Gallagher

REVIEW AND HERALD® PUBLISHING ASSOCIATION
HAGERSTOWN, MD 21740

Unless otherwise noted, Bible texts in this book are from the *Holy Bible,
New International Version.* Copyright © 1973, 1978, 1984, International Bible
Society. Used by permission of Zondervan Bible Publishers.
Bible texts credited to Phillips are from J. B. Phillips: *The New Testament
in Modern English,* Revised Edition. © J. B. Phillips 1958, 1960, 1972. Used by
permission of Macmillan Publishing Co., Inc.
Bible texts credited to TEV are from the *Good News Bible*—Old Testament:
Copyright © American Bible Society 1976; New Testament: Copyright ©
American Bible Society 1966, 1971, 1976.

This book was
Edited by Gerald Wheeler
Cover photo by PhotoDisc
Cover design by Helcio Deslandes
Typeset: Times 11/12

PRINTED IN U.S.A.

00 99 98 97 96   10 9 8 7 6 5 4 3 2 1

R&H Cataloging Service
Gallagher, Jonathan, 1952-
    The ultimate God.

    1. Bible. NT Epistles of John—Commentaries.   I. Title.

227.94

ISBN 0-8280-1272-5

Dedication

To Diny and Radmir
Two true friends of God

Contents

Introduction

The Essence
of Belief

The Epistles of John shine with the power and essence of belief. In their brief chapters we see what knowing and trusting God really means. Not some ethereal philosophy, not an academic exercise, but a deep, personal, practical trust in God described by one who knows Him intimately.

So who is this John who doesn't even need to sign his name? A man of God so well known that no one would ever question his authority as a church leader. Someone who saw the gospel go to the then-known world, who played his part in setting the Roman Empire upside down. This can be none other than the old apostle John himself—the disciple whom Jesus loved. Now, at the end of his life, he needs to write down his last thoughts. Brilliant, exciting, enthusiastic words on dramatic, spine-tingling themes flow from his mind—all written under inspiration by a man who is at least 80 (and more likely nearer 90) years old! John uses breathless words that fit the mind of a young visionary—but are more meaningful and telling when we know who wrote them, when, and why. Like his Lord, this former "son of thunder" uses simple yet profound words, delivered with total confidence.

My father wrote to me of his own conviction of the importance of these letters: "John's Epistles are striking reminders to me of how easy it is to lose touch with 'the simplicity which is toward Christ.' We need John's advice to be really living the Christian life day by day—'If we *say* and do not . . . , we lie,' but if we walk in the light, we have peace with God."

Totally direct, John writes out his summary of life's meaning and purpose. It is his "one-line definition of the gospel." The

Gospel of John is his major work. The Epistles, especially the first, are the "condensed version"—written in response to very clear needs. John meets error head-on, not in violence, but in love. He speaks absolutely straight to avoid any possibility of confusion. As Martin Luther said of 1 John: "I have never read a book written in simpler words than this one, and yet the words are inexpressible."

Why so? Because John has seen it all. He experienced firsthand the presence of God in Christ. After a long life as a persecuted Christian and a leader of the church, he is now the last disciple left alive. So with breathless flow of thought he links his ideas together, not as an exposition of a theme, but as an eyewitness trying to convey what he knows to be true. These are the mature thoughts of Jesus' beloved friend, who has pondered the good news Christ came to bring to humanity.

The apostle tries to explain the *meaning* of what he has seen and experienced, not just record events. So we can do no better than to consider very carefully what John wants us to know. For at the heart this is his spiritual last will and testament, his declaration of what is truly essential in God's glorious good news.

It's as if someone had come to the aged disciple for a last interview, asking, "So, John, what is most important in these beliefs of yours? Give me the gospel in a nutshell!" He cuts out everything not absolutely necessary and gives us a wonderful and inspiring vision of God and His gracious gift of salvation. Try the same challenge. If someone asked you to sum up in just a few words what God means to you, how would you answer? Take time to think about this, as John obviously has done, and write out a brief answer.

So read John's vital messages for us. Not just a few verses at a time. Read all the Letters—they're very short. Let the God whom John loved and admired speak to you personally.

The Word of Life

1

Death and life

When my wife's mother was dying, we were called to her bedside. By this time she was unconscious, and all we could do was to hold her hands and speak words of love and comfort, not knowing whether she was aware of us or not.

As the end came, we spoke of her last words of love to us and the family, of her regret at not being able to share in her children's lives any longer, but most of all, of her unshakable confidence in the salvation of her loving Lord. In her last days she had read and reread the Psalms, finding them particularly helpful as she battled the cancer that was taking over her body. Most of all, I remember her repeating the opening words of Psalm 27: "The Lord is my light and my salvation—whom shall I fear? The Lord is the stronghold of my life—of whom shall I be afraid?" (verse 1).

She died in peace and safety, secure in the arms of the God she knew and trusted as her very best friend. For when it comes right down to it, what do we live for? What is the point of all our fussing and fighting? What is our life, and where does it take us?

My mother-in-law had found the right answer and, like John, made sure her last words were full of meaning, practical, and relevant. "Only God, only God," she would say, half under her breath.

John's last words

So what of John's Epistles, written close to the end of his life? His last words are truly significant. Having had a lifetime to think about his experiences with Christ and His followers, he gives his explanation about what they all meant. After all, the aging apostle had had the most opportunity to reflect on the meaning of Christ's coming—His life, death, and resurrection.

From John's Gospel we learn of Jesus, the Eternal Word, the preexistent God who is at the Father's side and who has made Him known (see John 1:1-18). John records that "God so loved the world that he gave his one and only Son" (John 3:16). Why? Because "the one who comes from heaven is above all. He testifies to what he has seen and heard. . . . For the one whom God has sent speaks the words of God. . . . Whoever believes in the Son has eternal life" (verses 31-36).

From John we hear Jesus proclaim: "When a man believes in me, he does not believe in me only, but in the one who sent me. When he looks at me, he sees the one who sent me" (John 12:44, 45). "If you really knew me, you would know my Father as well. From now on, you do know him and have seen him" (John 14:7).

John reveals to us amazing statements of the truth about God and how He wants to relate to us: "I no longer call you servants, because a servant does not know his master's business. Instead, I have called you friends, for everything that I learned from my Father I have made known to you" (John 15:15). "I am not saying that I will ask the Father on your behalf. No, the Father himself loves you because you have loved me and have believed that I came from God" (John 16:26, 27).

How glad we should be for his inspired insights! Our image of the nature of God would be immeasurably poorer without the words he wrote down—words that even at the end of his life are vibrant with God's living power.

Breathless excitement in God

Just read again how he begins his First Epistle. One long, breathless sentence. *We* have heard! *We* have seen with our own eyes! *We* have looked at! *Our* hands have touched!

Any mistake here about the message he is trying to get across? I hardly think so! The apostle echoes here the beginning of his Gospel, in which he describes the Word that was from the beginning. But in his Gospel John attempted to get across the eternal divinity of Christ. Here John is making sure we don't miss the physical reality of the person of Jesus Christ (something that some were denying, saying Christ did not actually live on earth with a physical body).

"We were there!" he proclaims. "Each of us, His disciples, saw Jesus with our own eyes. We heard Him; we even touched Him. He was real, no doubt about it." Jesus was an absolutely real, physical person whom His followers had seen and physically touched, whom they had lived together with, and whom they had seen crucified and then resurrected. Without this, Christian belief has no basis.

I know Jesus

So starting right where it is essential to begin, John stands up and shouts out his message—I know this Jesus! I am the material eyewitness. And what I'm telling you is absolutely true, vindicated by the evidence of His life and what has happened since. Faith must be based on such evidence if it is not to be led astray.

Yet Jesus was no ordinary man, John continues. He is the *Word of Life*—a wonderful shorthand term that the disciple fills with meaning. He is the Word (remember what he said in the first chapter of his Gospel) and the Life. Of course, John is only reflecting the words of Jesus Himself: "I am the resurrection and the life" (John 11:25); "I have come that they may have life, and have it to the full" (John 10:10).

Jesus was God made manifest in human form, John declares. While truly Jesus was real, a complete and total human being in the flesh (and John is at pains to emphasize this, as we shall see later), yet He was also God.

John's vital message is this—why did Jesus come? To reveal God in all His fullness. All God's former attempts to communicate could be misunderstood. After all, He had transmitted them through fallen human beings. But this Being is God Himself, revealing in the clearest way possible who God is, what He is like, what His intentions are toward us, and the depths of His saving love.

The apostle's astounding theme is that the very God who spoke life into existence in Genesis 1 is this same Jesus.

"The life appeared," John continues, "we have seen it and testify to it, and we proclaim to you the eternal life, which was with the Father and has appeared to us" (1 John 1:2).

The person we know as Jesus is eternal life. A strange statement, but absolutely true. Jesus is not only the giver of eternal life; He *is* eternal life.

Reading the last page

Have you ever sneaked a look at the last page of a book to find out how things will work out? Reading ahead helps you to know what's going to happen. You see the end before you get there.

Each one of us has the privilege of reading the end of the book— the book of human history, the book of time, the book of life. God lets us discover how it will all work out. With Jesus we can be part of that end in a positive way, sharing together with Him in eternal life.

That's the vital truth Mum, my mother-in-law, had learned. It's the thought that drew her onward, that led her toward the reality of an incredible future with this Word of Life. If you're dying, what do you want to know? About the very opposite of what you are experiencing. The future becomes so much more important, because the present has so little to offer. The Word of Life is the transforming power of God that turns our feeble little lives here into a brilliant and fulfilled future life together with Him. That's why we joyfully read of the future when "the dwelling of God is with men, and he will live with them. They will be his people, and God himself will be with them and be their God" (Rev. 21:3).

But you only want that to happen if you know and trust this God who is the Word of Life now. Who wants to spend eternity with a tyrannical, hostile, or cruel God? Only as God is revealed in Jesus do we see that we have nothing to fear from the great Creator of the universe. Why? Because "this life became visible, we saw it" (1 John 1:2, TEV)—and we recognize in Jesus the true character of God as He really is. God has demonstrated that we have nothing to fear from Him.

Why Jesus came

Jesus came to show us God in the clearest way possible so that we would truly want to love Him and wish to be saved in His eternal kingdom. Only by love is love awakened, and that is what Jesus needed to do. Not to threaten or condemn, but to show us the outstretched arms of a God who was willing to be totally vulnerable, to die at our hands to show us His self-sacrificing love.

The Old Testament contains many descriptions of the way God deals with humanity. But they are not enough. Even the holiest of prophets cannot reveal the completeness of God and His nature. So

God had to come and show us Himself what He is like. God works, not through claims of goodness and promises of love, but through a *demonstration* of all that He is.

A wife may say in response to her husband's declarations of love: "Prove it!" Jesus, the Word of Life, is God proving it.

God became flesh and dwelt among us, John explains, so that we could, if we opened our eyes, recognize the truth about God. He even went to the extent of being born in a stable, raised by a peasant family, and working as a helper in a carpenter's shop. Beaten and abused, He was eventually crucified. God became totally involved with human existence—and John, who understood what he was seeing, declares: "We speak of it and tell you about the eternal life which was with the Father and was made known to us" (1 John 1:2, TEV).

Grabbing attention

So John grabs our attention and makes sure we see the vital importance of understanding what he has to say. He is the man with the qualifications to discuss Jesus, and he is talking about matters that are truly life and death.

John is the disciple
  a. whom Jesus loved.
  b. who stood at the foot of the cross—the only one.
  c. who had the longest Christian experience.
  d. who had the greatest understanding of God as we see demonstrated in his Gospel.
  e. who was the most respected leader ("the elder").

So because of who he is alone we should be listening to him intently. And when he begins with such an explosive introduction, how can we just sit there and not care what he is going to share with us?

We need to sit up and take notice! Why?

Because our eternal destiny is at stake—along with those around us. Which is why John himself is so persuasive—he sees how important his divinely inspired message really is.

So let's go right back to the beginning—the very beginning— and put the message in context.

The great controversy perspective helps us to understand that our world is the universe's lesson book and that we are a demon-

11

stration of this conflict's principles to both fellow human beings and angels (see 1 Cor. 4:9). God stands accused by Satan (a name meaning "accuser") of being unfit to govern the universe. The challenge facing God is to demonstrate His true nature in opposition to the devil's charges that He is dictatorial, hostile, power-crazed, unjust, arbitrary, cruel, severe, unloving, and so on. God wishes to show that He does not lay demands upon His created beings that He is unwilling to comply with Himself. So He comes as one of us:

- to show the eternal validity of the law as an expression of God's eternal goodness and righteousness.
- to represent the true character of God, especially as a God of love.
- to make known the truth of God to a fallen world.
- to represent the Father correctly, answering the misrepresentations of Satan that God is without mercy and patience, full of revenge.
- to make clear that God is not an arbitrary judge, delighting in condemning and punishing humanity.
- not only to tell the gospel, but to *be* the gospel by representing God in character.
- to reveal God's goodness—in mercy, tenderness, compassion, long-suffering, and self-sacrificing love.

Ultimately, all that we need to know—or even can know—of God stands revealed in the life and character of Jesus Christ.

Eyewitness

So what is John an eyewitness of? And why is this important? John is the last of the inner circle of people who stood closest to the earthly Jesus. He wants to make his position very clear—because already some are confusing the issue and turning the physical, real Jesus into some "spiritualized" figure. That's why John is so determined to reject such ideas—because he wants to convey the truth that he knew Jesus, not as some "figure of faith," but as a real and very close personal friend in the flesh.

So he says: "What we have seen and heard we announce to you also, so that you will join with us in the fellowship that we have with the Father and with his Son Jesus Christ" (1 John 1:3, TEV).

The apostle is totally convinced from personal experience who Jesus was. Now he writes because he has to convince those who have not had such a personal relationship with the bodily Jesus. Nothing makes an impact like a personal conviction. John is telling his audience that while some may have other ideas about Jesus, believe me, *I know! I was there!* The experience of being with Jesus and seeing God in Him totally changed his life. He wants to transmit this belief, this conviction, to the next generation.

Each generation faces the same challenge. Our objective is to pass on, not dry, dusty doctrines, cultural ideas, and social behaviors, but a true vision of the risen Lord and Saviour. You cannot force or manipulate it, but in some way every member must find the motivation to discover Jesus personally. We are only "church" as we can identify with Jesus as the God we love and the friend we want in our lives—now and forever.

That is why John declares: "We write this in order that our joy may be complete" (verse 4, TEV). What is true joy? Knowing that others share our understanding of God and love Him as we do.

Think of what this must have meant for John. Perhaps he wondered whether as the other disciples—"friends of Jesus"—passed off the scene the church would flounder and fail to hold to the truth about God of which he was so convinced. He must have felt a tremendous sense of responsibility. Surely he prayed that he had "said it right!"—that he had depicted the Christ he loved in a clear and convincing manner.

Then came the wonderful realization that others knew and loved this same Jesus, even though they had never met Him in the flesh! John's joy surely became complete as at the end of his life he saw so many believers in so many parts of the world who knew Jesus as he did.

The Word of Life is the living voice of God. John's testimony worked—and through the power of God we find ourselves changed into true friends of our loving Lord.

I asked Rebekah, age 9, what she thought of God—what she knew about what He is like. Here is the answer she wrote out—another tribute to God that would surely have warmed John's heart:

"God is mighty, loving, caring, kind, gracious, beautiful, right, good, true, friendly, humble, a king, the Saviour, the Creator, wonderful, and very close to me. I love God for making me me."

Thank you, Rebekah.—Love, Dad.

Light Against the Darkness

2

Lost in the dark

At 4.30 in the dark morning of Thursday, November 15, 1928, the coast guards at Rye in Sussex, England, received a message that the steamer *Alice Riga* was leaking and adrift off Dungeness. The alarm sounded, and the volunteers raced to the lifeboat station and launched the *Mary Stanford*.

An open lifeboat powered only by oars, the *Mary Stanford* was dragged down the beach into the huge waves and gale-force winds, and launched into the darkness. Its 17-man crew struggled to row the vessel out past the breakers and toward the drifting steamer.

Minutes later word came through that the *Alice Riga* was safe, and the recall signal sounded. But in the crashing seas none of the lifeboat crew heard the vital call to return. And in the oppressive darkness of that night they could not see at all.

At midday someone sighted the *Mary Stanford* floating upside down, and the bodies of the crewmen began to wash ashore. All 17 were lost, and the memorial at the lifeboat station records their names. Some were from the same family—father and sons, or brothers perhaps—and one family lost three. What a tragedy to a waiting family to realize that three of their menfolk had been lost at the same time.

And the tragedy is doubly tragic, for their heroic sacrifice had been unnecessary. They had been trying to save a ship that was safe, and had lost their own lives in the process.

14

No one has used the lonely lifeboat house on the shingle shore since that disastrous day. It stands as a silent witness on the windswept coast to the courage of those who sought to save others and yet were themselves shipwrecked.

The deserted building is a powerful reminder of Paul's words, that in seeking to save others we should not risk making a castaway of our own faith. If only the coast guards had heard the recall. If only the message had come sooner. If only it had not been on such a dark and stormy night.

Lost in the darkness. A terrible and tragic fate, but one that mirrors the spiritual destiny of many today. How many of our own lives are filled with "if onlys"? If only we had listened to God's call to repent. If only we had responded to His offer of salvation. If only we had chosen to follow His way.

Playing games?

Many of us are truly "lost in the dark." Like frightened children, we are afraid of the dark, yet refuse to come "out of darkness into his wonderful light" (1 Peter 2:9). Like children, we play games in which we blindfold ourselves so we deliberately prevent ourselves from seeing.

Spiritual games are the most dangerous. Phillips puts 1 John 1:6 this way: "Consequently, if we were to say that we enjoyed fellowship with him and still went on living in darkness, we should be both telling and living a lie."

By refusing to love the light, we live the lie. For if we truly love God, we live in His light, as John so strongly declares: "God is light; in him there is no darkness at all" (verse 5). God has no shadow of darkness, no blemish of evil, no seed of sin. Light defines God; it is His nature; it tells us who He is.

So what is the light that is God?

Light

Light is what enables us to see anything at all. It is energy that eradicates darkness. Spiritual light gives us understanding and freedom from fear, and helps us to understand how God operates the universe. Light is knowledge that sets us free.

But, as in the case of time and many other important things, attempt to define what light is, and you're into major problems!

We can measure the speed of physical light: 186,000 miles per second—the theoretical speed limit of the universe. And according to the theory of relativity, funny things happen when you approach that speed—such as mass becoming infinite. In other words, the faster you go, the more massive you become. This is odd stuff, the physics of relativity. We can measure light's intensity and wavelength, and we are all aware of its importance and its effects.

But when you ask what light is, you encounter answers that are more intriguing than informative. "It's an energy waveform," says one physicist. "Occurring at different wavelengths, it is just part of the electromagnetic spectrum." Fine. So it's like some kind of energy wave. But ask another physicist (or even the same one!) and you're told, "Light is made up of particles similar to subatomic particles in the way they behave. There's even a name for these particles—photons."

Clear enough? Light is a wave and a particle. Yes, and both at the same time. And that's just the simple stuff.

Truly weird science, but intriguing enough to make you think, I hope. That Scripture defines God as light is perhaps even more meaningful as scientists explore and examine the phenomenon and find more questions than answers.

And what of this vast universe, measured in units based on how long light travels in a year? What of the Creator God and the very beginning when He said, "Let there be light, and there was light"?

God as light

If we define God as light, we must remember that He is also the Creator of light. God wraps Himself in a garment of light (see Ps. 104:2). He is the very essence of light—in all its meanings of seeing and understanding. God's truth illuminates the pathways of our lives (see Ps. 119:105). David proclaims: "The Lord is my light" (Ps. 27:1).

But perhaps the most powerful image is from Jesus, who declares: "I am the light of the world" (John 8:12; cf. 9:5). John's emphasis on Jesus as the light is one of the hallmarks of his theology—his understanding of God. Twenty-four times in his Gospel John refers to light. In the first chapter he describes the

Word as the light of humanity, the light that shines in ... the true light that illuminates every person in the world. W... the purpose of the light? It was to illuminate God in the midst of h... manity, to make Him known (see John 1:18).

And John 3 makes the relationship of evil to that light plain— people hate the light because those who wish to carry on in their wickedness prefer darkness. "But whoever lives by the truth comes into the light" (John 3:21).

We belong to the light

That's why Jesus appeals: "You are going to have the light just a little while longer. Walk while you have the light, before darkness overtakes you. The man who walks in the dark does not know where he is going. Put your trust in the light while you have it, so that you may become sons of light" (John 12:35, 36). We need to become children of light, for that is what Scripture says we now are in Jesus. As children of the day we belong to the light (see 1 Thess. 5:5) because we belong to the God of light.

When Jesus tells the people, "I have come into the world as a light, so that no one who believes in me should stay in darkness" (John 12:46), He is truly claiming to be God—the God of light, of revelation, of illumination.

So God is light. Jesus is light. That blinding light illuminates the world so that we can see where we're going and who we are. By shining into our hearts and driving back the darkness of sin, light reveals what is wrong with us. It also shows us the way we should walk in life. Like a lighthouse, it flashes out a beacon of hope and warning to all who will see.

But that is not enough. It's not sufficient to say "Look, there is a light" and do nothing about it. We can ignore the light. Once we realize that God is light and that Jesus is our light, we need to step out from the shadows into its rays. Only then, as we enter that blazing radiance, can the God of light do anything for us. God calls us out of the darkness into His wonderful light (see 1 Peter 2:9). *We need to move*—we can't just stay where we are. Just as moths head toward a bright window, we need to fly toward God. God's light calls us to Him. If we don't respond, He can't help us.

So what are we to do? Accept the light and walk toward it. In fact, we are to walk *in* the light: that is, we share and participate in the light as we live our lives in accordance with its illuminating rays (see 1 John 1:7). Not only that, but the light must also transform us. We can't remain the same as we once were—we need to let God's light fill us and change us.

Think of yourself as photographic film. Before we expose film to light it has no image, no picture. When we load it into a camera and press the shutter, it records what the light reveals at that moment. The chemicals of the film change, and after we develop it we find a perfect image of that light. By beholding we become changed. Looking face-to-face with Jesus, the author and finisher of our faith, we discover ourselves becoming more and more like Him. And so we find ourselves transformed into sons and daughters of the light.

"For you were once darkness, but now you are light in the Lord. Live as children of light" (Eph. 5:8).

Now you are what? *Light in the Lord.* How should we live? *As children of light.* Where do we belong? *To the light, to the God of light.* And having accepted this light, having become children of this marvelous light, having known the Light of the world, what also do we become?

The lights of the world ourselves. Jesus told us, His light-filled disciples, "You are the light of the world. . . . . Let your light shine" (Matt. 5:14-16).

Once we were darkness, but now we are light. We hardly need reminding that day and night are opposites, so we should have nothing to do with spiritual darkness (see 2 Cor. 6:14). "We do not belong to the night or to the darkness. So then let us not be like others who are asleep, but let us be alert and self-controlled" (1 Thess. 5:6).

The blind and deaf writer Helen Keller described her experience: "I can see, and that is why I can be so happy, in what you call the dark, but which to me is golden. I can see a God-made world, not a manmade world."

Lying claims

Those who say they belong to the light should offer solid evidence of their new state for others to see. John describes three lying claims, ones many still try to make today.

Claim 1. What I do doesn't affect my spirituality (see 1 John 1:6). Here the idea is that while the body is sinful, the spirit is pure. So what I *actually* do is not the important question, say such pseudo-Christians. But John will have nothing of such a lying claim. If we are truly children of light, he says, then we will live good and honest Christian lives in fellowship with one another, not thinking we are part of some "spiritual elite."

And what of those who claim to be such spiritual elitists and yet exhibit unchristian behavior? I have always believed that once you resort to methods and actions that do not represent God's character, then you have lost the truth no matter how "right" you may be. Correct theology reveals itself more in the behavior of the theologian than in some theological treatise. This is what John wants to make plain: right ideas mean right actions, or as one famous preacher put it: "You can't think crooked and live straight."

Claim 2. I don't sin (see 1 John 1:8), or I'm not a sinner. I well remember the reaction of my landlady when I was a student studying away from home in Birmingham, England. I'd put up a Christian poster in my window, something about God calling all sinners to repentance. Horrified, she asked me to take it down. In the zeal of youth I refused, saying we were all sinners in need of repentance.

"Me, a sinner?" she asked incredulously. "I'm not a sinner. I've not stolen things or murdered anybody. I'm sure I'm not a sinner!"

Such an attitude is commonplace today. Many people cannot see themselves as sinners in need of God's transforming grace. They identify themselves as "quite good people, really" and do not recognize their need for healing from their sin-sick lives. But as Phillips puts it: "If we refuse to admit that we are sinners, then we live in a world of illusion and truth becomes a stranger to us" (1 John 1:8). We need to be purified (verses 7, 9)—an action that the verb tense John uses indicates is an ongoing process, not something that happens once and is finished with.

Claim 3. I haven't sinned. This is the doctrine of spiritual infallibility (see 1 John 1:10).

If we say we haven't sinned, obviously we have no need of a Saviour. Rejecting God's forgiveness, we deny both our own characters and God's and turn Him into a liar when He says that we do need a deliverer.

The truth is that the closer we come to God, the more we see our own deficiencies and imperfections. We have nothing to boast about except, as Paul says, the cross of Christ. Claims of sinlessness mean nothing. All that really matters is our relationship to God and how *He* sees us, not what we claim for ourselves or others.

God identifies us as sinful beings, a fact that we cannot deny (see Rom. 3:10, 23; Isa. 64:6). He is concerned to tell us about our sinfulness, not to be hostile or unforgiving, but so that He can do something about it. In so many ways God is the divine physician who pleads with us to choose life, to come to Him and receive His healing salvation: "Turn! Turn from your evil ways! Why will you die, O house of Israel?" (Eze. 33:11).

We need to give up our pretense and expose our true nature to the light of God's revealing truth. God comes with His searchlight of truth, banishing our spiritual darkness as He seeks all those lost in the night of evil and sin.

So are you still in the dark? Are you outside of the powerful beams of that searchlight of truth, unwilling to stand in its brightness? Are you still hesitating to come out of darkness into God's wonderful light?

Remember the *Mary Stanford* and its lost crew. "Today, if you hear his voice, do not harden your hearts" (Ps. 95:7, 8). Before you shipwreck in the storm of evil—even if you are trying to do good—listen to the Lord and come to Him. Come to the Jesus who says to the winds and the waves that threaten to overwhelm our fragile little boats, "Peace, be still," and who will guide us through, safe and sound, to the heavenly shore.

We belong to the light.

1 John 2:1-11

Walking Like Jesus

3

Theories and evidence

Ever heard of phlogiston? Not many people have today. But go back a couple hundred years, and phlogiston was all the rage. So what exactly is (or was) phlogiston?

Phlogiston is something you can't see or touch or feel. It's a kind of invisible element that moves between substances when they burn. So when something burns, it loses phlogiston to the air or whatever it's burning in. Clear? Oh, and it has negative weight!

In other words, the more phlogiston something contains, the less it weighs. So as it burns, it loses the phlogiston, with its negative weight, and becomes heavier. Clearer now?

And has anybody ever identified this mysterious phlogiston? No. Has anybody proposed a chemical formula? No. Are we even sure it exists? No.

But the chemists of the eighteenth century believed in it. They thought they had the evidence. Observing what happened when things burned, they decided that the theory of phlogiston made sense of what they were seeing.

Nowadays we can smile at such a foolish belief. But back then it was good science. The chemists thought they had the proof they needed. And once someone had claimed phlogiston as the magic substance, scientifically proven, then others went along with the concept—for more than 100 years. Chemist and church minister Joseph Priestley even managed to discover oxygen, but was so full of the theory that he called it "dephlogisticated air."

So what of our spiritual "theories"? Do they make any more

sense than the mythical phlogiston? What is the proof behind what we say we believe in? We may make many claims for our spiritual experience, but what are such claims really worth?

John forces us back to the evidence—the evidence of true Christianity in action. What point is there in any great claim of personal piety if our actions demonstrate that we are liars? "The man who says, 'I know him,' but does not do what he commands is a liar, and the truth is not in him" (1 John 2:4). In this sense there can be no such thing as "theoretical Christianity." On the contrary, Christianity is essentially a very *practical* religion. Whatever you may claim, it's what you do that counts, John declares.

Who's telling the truth?

So how do we deal with such claims and counterclaims? How can we really know who's telling the truth? Only by making sure we examine the evidence, see the results, recognize the practical outcomes.

Lies and the truth, claims and counterclaims—we need good judgment to discern the difference. But in the end (maybe not until the very end) the truth will out. Until then we must not be spiritually blind, and without being judgmental, we must examine those who make religious claims by the fruit they grow in their lives. For as John says, "This is how we know we are in him: whoever claims to live in him must walk as Jesus did" (verses 5, 6).

So while many groups around us, both inside and outside the church, may *say* they know God, it is only as they reflect a Christlike spirit in their lives that we can be sure they're telling the truth.

The two surefire tests that John points to as examples of walking like Jesus are:

1. "We know that we have come to know him if we obey his commands" (verse 3)

2. "Whoever loves his brother lives in the light, and there is nothing in him to make him stumble" (verse 10).

In the same way that Jesus did not destroy the law but rather fulfilled it in His life and teachings, so are we to live. Any Christian who says that we no longer need to keep God's commands is not living like Christ. Of course, we do need to realize that God has commanded different actions at different times, as the early church recognized. We no longer need to practice circumcision as a religious rite, for example, or observe the ceremonial days or the Old Testament sacrificial system. But the basic commands enshrined in the Ten Commandments remain valid, for they reflect God as He is. We follow them not as a legalistic practice, but as an expression of our love for God, showing that we delight to do His will.

The other test of love for each other reminds us of Jesus' own "command": "A new command I give you: Love one another. As I have loved you, so you must love one another" (John 13:34). "If you love me, you will obey what I command" (John 14:15; see also John 15:12, 17).

Of course, love cannot be "commanded." It is a principle that flows from freedom and choice, and as we choose God and His way, then we respond out of love. "We love because he first loved us" (1 John 4:19).

Commands?

The idea of love for one another goes right back through the Old Testament. Love for one's neighbor, love for God—Jesus' summary of the Ten Commandments—is not new either. Yet as John thinks about this (1 John 2:7, 8) he realizes that there is a new element. The newness is the arrival of Jesus Himself. For though God has demonstrated His love through the ages and has always wished love to be the determining principle of behavior, until Jesus came, God had not been able to demonstrate it to the fullest.

Now we view this new "command" in all its glory—in the life and especially the death of Jesus. "Its truth is seen in him and you, because the darkness is passing and the true light is already shining" (verse 8).

Notice also the "and you" in that verse. God's wonderful love is not only demonstrated in Jesus; it is also revealed in us as we choose to love. We are God's witnesses, His examples, in this fallen world—we are a demonstration to angels and to human beings (see 1 Cor. 4:9).

Walking like Jesus

So we must walk as Jesus walked. The Bible writers used the imagery of walking to describe how one lived. When the Bible says

23

to walk in Jesus, we must pay careful attention. That's why it is so important to spend time reading the Gospels. We need to know how Jesus behaved, what His speech was like, how He treated people.

Our study is not as a way of "copying" Jesus in terms of salvation—believing that "if He can do it, so can we." Jesus did not come to *show* us the recipe of salvation; He came to *be* our salvation. He simply demonstrates to us the kind of life we should lead, in full agreement with the will of God.

"I wonder what Jesus would have done in this situation?" is a question some frequently ask. It has its merits in trying to recognize goodness and truth. Yet we must recognize that we are not Jesus. The temptations He faced were those designed for a divine being (we have, for example, no temptation to turn stones into bread. Nor does the devil offer us kingship of the whole world—he knows most of us would settle for much less than that!). Jesus was unique, and we must see in Him not only a good and righteous man living a correct life, but also God in human form. Never should we downplay the divinity of Christ simply so we can make Jesus our "perfect example of a man to follow."

In walking as Jesus did, showing that we are true sons and daughters of God, we must have the same kind of attitudes and thoughts that Jesus expressed. That's the kind of "walking like Jesus" John is speaking of. The principles of love, kindness, goodness, compassion, honesty, truthfulness, and so on must mark our lives as they did that of Jesus. Most of all, we need to remember that Jesus was revealing the true nature and character of God to us, and that we are required to reveal the same God to those around us. As we have the love for each other that God intended, then, Jesus says, everyone will know we are His disciples (see John 13:35).

Dealing with sin

But sadly, unlike Jesus, we still do sin. John recognizes this fact: "My dear children, I write this to you so that you will not sin. But if anybody does sin, we have one who speaks to the Father in our defense—Jesus Christ, the Righteous One" (1 John 2:1).

Immediately we need to be careful here. When the text says that Jesus Christ speaks to the Father in our defense, does that mean that the Father is the accuser, or that He loves us less than the Son?

In no way. In trying to speak well of the Son, sometimes we have spoken less than well of the Father. To suggest in some way that God is hostile toward us goes against Scripture, especially the words of Jesus when He tells us that the Father loves us Himself in the same way as the Son (see John 16:27, etc).

Who is the accuser? Satan—whose name means the accuser. So when we think of how God deals with us, even in our sinfulness, let us be very careful not to split the Godhead and suggest that one member of the Trinity has to persuade Another to grant forgiveness to us. It was *because* of the love of God that Jesus came and died to save us, not as a way of trying to make God love us as a result.

A billboard advertised a recent action movie: "Crime is the disease—meet the cure." To paraphrase that slogan: "Sin is the disease—meet the cure, Jesus Christ!"

God provides the *means* to forgive our sins. He is the *remedy* for sin. Jesus *makes us one* (at-one-ment) with God once more. How much easier to understand this than archaic words such as propitiation! (To include in the meaning of such a word the suggestion that in some way Jesus is "buying off" or "placating" the Father is to accept the devil's picture of God's nature and to split the Trinity asunder.)

Rather this is part of God's open government. The devil, not God, is humanity's accuser. And it is Jesus who speaks on our behalf before God as righteous judge, and the whole universe then sees the "rightness" of God's decisions.

In John 16:26 Jesus says that He will *not* ask the Father on our behalf. Why not? Because the Father loves us as much as the Son and is just as willing to save us! Through the plan of redemption, which involves all three members of the Godhead, the Trinity reconciles and brings us back to God, sets us right, and keeps us right by Him. For "Christ himself is the means by which our sins are forgiven, and not our sins only, but also the sins of everyone" (1 John 2:2, TEV).

What an incredible God—One who was willing to sacrifice so much to win us back to Himself! As He deals with sin, God demonstrates the eternal validity of truth and right, as well as His loving, saving nature. The cross of Christ reveals the whole character of God in all its glory.

God and His evidence

God was not satisfied with making claims and arguing with the devil and his charges against the nature and government of God. Rather, He wished to reject Satan's claims by clear and unmistakable evidence.

In the same way, "anyone who *claims* to be in the light but hates his brother is still in the darkness" (verse 9). We can all make claims, say wonderful things, but the proof, the evidence, is in our attitudes and actions.

So what are you going to do? Are you willing to examine your own life and see how it matches up to such an investigation? What evidence are you displaying? What of you and your spiritual destiny? For whatever your *claims*, God is interested only in demonstration. "Whoever *claims* to live in him must walk as Jesus did" (verse 6).

Manufacturers make many claims for their products. The ads declare their benefits. Whose promises do you believe? How do you know they are true? By looking at consumer reports. By talking to others who have firsthand experience. But best of all, by checking for yourself—taking a test-drive, experimenting with a sample, making use of a trial period. You need to be sure. "This is how we can be sure that we are in union with God: whoever says that he remains in union with God should live just as Jesus Christ did" (verses 5, 6, TEV).

1 John 2:12-17

What Knowing
God Means

4

Making deals with God?

I happened to be visiting a church member in the hospital when the woman in the next bed asked me to speak to her privately. Explaining that she'd heard me speaking about God, she wanted to ask me something.

She said that she had experienced a massive stroke. The doctors were gravely concerned for her, especially should she suffer a second stroke. They had already warned her that the first stroke would affect her permanently, and indeed she had great difficulty talking. Her question was that if she should give all her money to God, would He cure her?

Smiling, I told her that wasn't the way God worked. I tried to share my understanding of who God is and what He is like. But she didn't seem to take much in, as if she had already made her decision about what she was going to do. At the end she told me, "I'm going to give all I have to God, and I know He will heal me. I have plenty of money—God will respect that. I'm going to go to church, and He'll see I'm sincere. Pray for me."

And I did pray. She reminded me of so many others—trying to make deals with God. Whatever it is we value, in extreme situations we will promise it all to God. "Just get me out of this, God, and I'll do anything You want. Just help me *now*."

At least the prayer of the downed flier in the North Sea during

World War II was honest: "God, I haven't bothered You for the past 30 years. If You get me out of this, I won't bother You for the next 30, either."

But even here there's the idea of some kind of deal. As if we have anything to bargain with. Does God really want your money or fame or talents if they're just "bargaining chips"?

Or there's the other extreme—from a church member with gray hair who told me: "It doesn't matter if God likes me or I like God. That's got nothing to do with it. I've done what God requires. I've kept my side of the bargain. So God *has* to let me into heaven, because I've done what I was told."

How's that for the assurance of salvation? He was absolutely convinced, too—he saw it as just a question of contract: I do my part; God has to do His part!

Maybe we all have some of that mentality inside us. When something bad strikes, we are on our knees making all kinds of promises. We talk about paying double tithes and fasting and taking church office and so on. Or we recall all the sacrifices we have made "for God," which should gain us some merit with Him. We talk about all the times we wanted to sin but didn't because we didn't want to forfeit our reward. Surely we should get some credit for all the good things we've done, right? All those years of observing the Sabbath, of contributing our money, of serving the church, of healthy living, of avoiding bad places of entertainment, of keeping the commandments . . .

As if we would have lived very differently if we'd had the choice! But viewing God as a divine police officer, we believed He surely would catch us, and then we would have been in trouble. The Pharisees perfected this system. By assuming that through doing good and avoiding evil they gained credit with God, they eventually missed seeing Him in Christ—because He was not the God they had their "contract" with. Tragedy of tragedies, they (and we can do the same) crucified the Lord of glory for claiming to be God. Why? Because Jesus Christ rejected their ideas of making deals, and appealed for a direct, personal relationship of healing salvation.

We can never make deals with God.

But the woman patient made her promises anyway. And miraculously, it seemed, she recovered well.

Did she keep her bargain? Sadly, no. She never went near a church, nor did she give anything to God. For now she was better, and the doctors were pleased and said she'd done well. She didn't need God anymore, she reasoned.

Giving up on God?

The tragedy of today's world is that so many have given up on God without really knowing who He is. Often when I ask atheists to tell me about the kind of God they don't believe in, I agree with what they say! The devil's misrepresentations have led many to spurn a wrong picture of God, one that we also would reject. Without a knowledge of the true character of God, we can never have a loving response to Him. The task for us, then, is to make God known as He truly is—full of goodness, mercy, and truth. The last message of mercy to our dying world is a revelation of God's loving character.

One contemporary singer tells of her disillusionment with God. Though she had been brought up in a Christian home, the odd religious language and customs seemed strange. But what really turned her against God was the preaching of "hellfire and brimstone." She decided that if this was the kind of person God was, she didn't have any use for Him. And, she supposed, He probably didn't have any use for her. A tragic loss because of a terrible misrepresentation of the real truth about God and His attitudes and actions.

Others too have rejected such a torturing, vindictive, hostile God:

"The idea that a good God would send people to a burning hell is utterly damnable to me—the ravings of insanity, superstition gone to seed" (Luther Burbank).

"I do not myself feel that any person who is really profoundly human can believe in everlasting punishment. . . . I must say that I think all this doctrine, that hellfire is a punishment for sin, is a doctrine of cruelty" (Bertrand Russell).

"[Hell] makes man an eternal victim and God an eternal fiend. It is the one infinite horror. . . . Beyond this Christian dogma, savagery cannot go" (Robert Ingersoll).

"An eternally burning hell preached from the pulpit, and kept before the people, does injustice to the benevolent character of God. It presents Him as the veriest tyrant of the universe. This widespread dogma has turned thousands to universalism, infidelity, and atheism" (Ellen White).

One of those turned to such skepticism was the Robert Ingersoll quoted above. At the age of 10 he heard a sermon on the horrors of hell and said, "Father, if this is the kind of God the God in heaven is, I don't want any part of Him."

Hell comes from two lies. One was the lie Satan told in the garden: "You will not surely die" (Gen. 3:4). It is the basis for the belief in the immortal soul. The other lie is that God is vindictive, punitive, and cruel. Add the two lies together, and you have the concept of hell.

Remember that the author of hell is not God, but the devil. Hell is one of his best strategies to turn people away from God—just another part of his smear campaign to destroy the noble character of our loving God. As Francis Bacon wrote: "It were better to have no opinion of God at all than such an opinion as is unworthy of Him."

The tragedy is, of course, that once people give up on God, they are lost. "If people stop believing in God, they don't then believe in nothing, they believe in anything," wrote G. K. Chesterton.

That's why John commends the fathers in his churches ("because you have known him who is from the beginning" [1 John 2:13]), and the young men ("because . . . the word of God lives in you" [verse 14]). It's *absolutely essential* that we each one realize what knowing God really means. Our concept of God must be correct, for it shapes our spiritual relationship with Him. The kind of person we believe God to be affects every aspect of belief, and if we have a false concept of God, then it will seriously damage our spiritual relationship.

God concepts

So what of false concepts of God? Look at some thoughts about God from famous writers, and see if they do not reflect many popular but erroneous ideas about Him:

"God is what man finds that is divine in himself" (Max Lerner).

"Is man only a blunder of God, or God only a blunder of man?" (Friedrich Nietzsche).

"If God has created us in His image, we have repaid Him well" (Voltaire).

"It may be that our role on this planet is not to worship God—but to create Him" (Arthur C. Clarke).

"I've steered clear of God. He was an incredible sadist" (John Collier).

You can add to the list of concepts yourself. Vague energy clouds, some distant divine Watchmaker of the universe, a cosmic Santa Claus, the force of the cosmos, and so on—all these kinds of things have been identified with God.

But they represent the same kinds of ideas that John is combating here. Each of his six repetitions of "I write to you" (1 John 2:12-14) represents a particular aspect of spiritual understanding, and he lists "knowing God" in three of the "commendations." How important, then, that we rightly understand and relate to this God who has done so much at tremendous cost to make sure He is known!

Forgiveness and victory

"But I don't really feel it. I don't know whether God has done what I asked. I don't *feel* forgiven."

As we seek right ideas about God and His nature, we will also begin to wonder how He operates. Many times in my ministry I have had to speak to people who wanted forgiveness but did not know whether they were forgiven or not.

Sometimes they thought they needed to do some special penance. The human mind has the idea that you need to prove goodness or true contrition to God before He will listen to your cry for forgiveness. Some do not seem to be able to accept the graciousness of God, and though they read the texts about God's willingness to forgive, somehow they just cannot believe.

If you have ever thought like this, read again what John is saying here: "Your sins are forgiven for the sake of Christ" (verse 12, TEV). No doubts here—the promise is sure and certain. Because of the revelation of God in Christ, you *know* that God can and will forgive you as you come to Him in repentance and contrition. God does not need to be persuaded, nor placated with some offering, but is more willing to forgive than we are to ask. Remember what we have already read: "If we confess our sins, he is faithful and just and will forgive us our sins and purify us from all unrighteousness" (1 John 1:9).

When does it happen? The moment we ask! How can this happen? Because of the very nature of God Himself.

But don't miss something vital here. God, though He can and does forgive, desires to do even more. Notice the end of that text: "and purify us from all unrighteousness." What God wants is not to be always forgiving, but for us to allow Him to change us so that we no longer choose our sinful desires. God longs to make us new (see 2 Cor. 5:17). More than anything else He seeks to remake us in His image, to prepare us for an eternity together with Him. So though forgiveness is important, healing from our sinfulness is even more important. Because that is what brings spiritual victory!

The overcoming of the evil one (see 1 John 2:13) is just that. It is a rejection of the devil's lies, a forsaking of his way of living, a refusal of his temptations. It occurs not by our own strength, but by the transforming power of God at work in our lives, which turns us from rebellious enemies into trustworthy friends of God.

God's desire is to have a people who are more than simply "acquitted." To be pronounced legally not guilty, pardoned, and forgiven is one thing. But wonder of wonders, what God achieves is a people who will stand for right even though everything collapses around them, who are so settled into truth that nothing will budge them. They have been so totally convinced of the *rightness* of God that they would not choose to live any other way.

When the angel announced Jesus' birth, he called Him Jesus, not because He would *forgive* His people their sins, but because He would *save* His people *from* their sins! (see Matt. 1:21).

Even if we should refuse His help and eventually die, just as a doctor who goes to the funeral of a patient who rejected his or her aid, God may still be saying "I forgive you"—but we will be dead. Forgiveness can never be enough—it must lead us to that oneness with God that comes from the fact that "the word of God lives in you" (1 John 2:14).

Loving the world or living forever?

John is totally explicit in his command: "Do not love the world or anything that belongs to the world" (verse 15, TEV). With that direct order he goes on to explain that what our world regards as valuable is nothing—it is temporary and will soon be gone:

"Everything that belongs to the world—what the sinful self desires, what people see and want, and everything in this world that people are so proud of—none of this comes from the Father; it all comes from the world. The world and everything in it that people desire is passing away" (verses 15-17, TEV).

Really, it's not a question of liking or disliking certain "worldly" activities. Rather it's a question of deciding what is permanent and genuine and what is temporary and counterfeit. The decision is about what you truly value, what you truly live for.

Only by recognizing God as He is can we have a happy and fulfilled life now, and an eternity in His glorious presence. We need to come to grips with what knowing God means!

This Last Hour!

5

The spirit of antichrist

At 7:00 in the morning on January 26, 1984, Anthony Antone was executed. Convicted of arranging a murder, he went to the electric chair. Another death, another depressing statistic. But Antone's refusal to speak to a priest or have the services of a gospel minister distinguished this particular execution. In fact, he rejected Christianity altogether, calling such beliefs "childish."

Antone went to his death without hope, and seemingly without any thought of any possible future. In this we see the results of the work of antichrist, who has done so much to turn humanity away from God—to reject Him completely. To believe in God is a "crutch," many say, just a way of getting through life because you can't stand up for yourself. OK for kids, maybe, but not for adults.

But says John: "Any man who refuses to acknowledge the Father and the Son is the anti-christ" (1 John 2:22, Phillips). Or as Jesus said: "He who is not with me is against me" (Matt. 12:30).

Sometimes as we focus on the dramatic end-time revelation of antichrist we miss the meaning of what being "anti-Christian" really is. The word carries two major thoughts. The first is of being *against* Christ—that is, in opposition to Him and all He stands for. The second is of being *in place* of Christ—that is, as a substitute replacing Christ.

These two facets of antichrist clearly mark Satan's campaign to deceive and destroy. Today's society is against both the calls and claims of Christ, and also seeks to replace Christ and Christian philosophy with alternatives.

Against God through a society that looks for money and possessions.

Against God by direct attack through satanism and witchcraft.

Against God more subtly by making humanity indifferent to religion and any thought of a loving God.

Replacing God with "a good time," sex, drugs, alcohol.

Replacing God with a fake "god" in false religions.

Replacing God with false ideas about God, even within His church.

Lucifer: ever anti-God

This anti-God spirit has been present in God's universe ever since the rebellion of Lucifer. Presenting himself as some kind of "freedom fighter" battling for the "rights" of the intelligent beings of the universe, Lucifer has always intended to malign and destroy God. The fallen archangel has always been *anti*-Christ. He is *anti* everything that God represents: freedom, choice, love.

He stands behind the man of lawlessness described so vividly in 2 Thessalonians 2:3-9. Read it, for you need to know what he is doing so you will not be deceived by spurious miracles and divine claims! Note the particular characteristics of opposition to God and exaltation over God (the same traits Lucifer exhibited in the beginning; see Isa. 14 and Eze. 28).

No one uses the term *antichrist* in Scripture except John, and it occurs only in 1 and 2 John. But there's no mistaking the meaning. "Many deceivers, who do not acknowledge Jesus Christ as coming in the flesh, have gone out into the world. Any such person is the deceiver and the antichrist" (2 John 7).

"This is how you can recognize the Spirit of God: Every spirit that acknowledges that Jesus Christ has come in the flesh is from God, but every spirit that does not acknowledge Jesus is not from God. This is the spirit of the antichrist, which you have heard is coming and even now is already in the world" (1 John 4:2, 3).

In this John parallels Paul's use of the phrase "god of this world." "The god of this age has blinded the minds of unbelievers, so that they cannot see the light of the gospel of the glory of Christ, who is the image of God" (2 Cor. 4:4).

The deceptive, lying goal of the archdeceiver is to clothe God in demonic disguise. He seeks to portray God as hostile, arrogant, uncaring, unloving, merciless, and unforgiving. The end result? A world that neither sees God, nor cares whether it does or not. A mass of humanity that "cannot see the light of the gospel of the glory of Christ, *who is the image of God."*

The image of God

Don't miss that last point. It is John's great and ultimate thesis! "For whoever rejects the Son rejects also the Father; whoever accepts the Son has the Father also" (1 John 2:23, TEV).

Here John is simply repeating the wonderful words of Jesus that only he recorded:

"Whoever believes in me believes not only in me but also in him who sent me. Whoever sees me sees also him who sent me" (John 12:44, 45, TEV). " 'Now that you have known me,' he said to them, 'you will know my Father also, and from now on you do know him and you have seen him.' " "Whoever has seen me has seen the Father" (John 14:7, 9, TEV).

This last hour

As the final hour approaches, the spiritual battle heats up. The fundamental causes of the conflict between Christ and antichrist move toward the inevitable climax. The polarization of attitudes is there for all to see—even now.

The reasons for the great controversy at its beginning continue to its end. It is important, then, that we have eyes to see and ears to hear and minds to understand. Religion—and I mean all aspects of religious belief—is moving toward authoritarianism. The rise of fundamentalism in many religions is a drive toward unquestioning "obedience"—a rigorous observance of the requirements the leaders demand. Added to this is the generally conceded idea that religion does not need to make sense. Because religion deals with the supernatural, many apparently assume that we must then reject reason.

The trouble is, with so many voices claiming to speak for God, how does anyone find out who's telling the truth? Is it the voice that shouts loudest? the one that does the most miracles? the most attractive/appealing/seductive?

Few even seem to take the time to think about such questions. More than ever, we need the gift of spiritual discernment. We require not some vague feeling or some warm conviction, but hard and visible evidence. God is a God of evidence, and wishes us to make our decisions with the minds He has given us. The antichrist and all the subordinate antichrists do not want such thought, but mindless obedience, like the thought police of Orwell's *1984*.

Take a look at some of those who have both opposed and replaced Christ. Cult leaders provide dramatic illustrations of the drive for mind control. Cult organizations tell their members not to think for themselves. The leadership does that for them—they should just follow along, blindly and automatically. And we become cultic whenever we advise our fellow members to do the same. While it is right and proper to respect spiritual leaders, we must never rely solely on human beings to teach us what we should or should not believe. Beliefs such as the priesthood of all believers, individual responsibility, personal salvation, and so on should make us all aware that we must think and understand for ourselves. As Paul so clearly says: "Let every man be fully persuaded in his own mind" (Rom. 14:5, KJV).

We are not to depend upon a human teacher, however brilliant and charismatic, for our understanding of God and His wonderful plan of salvation. Instead, we are to be able to give a reason ourselves for our spiritual hope (see 1 Peter 3:15). As Matthew Henry remarked: "We should be able to defend our religion with meekness." This means we need to know the truth personally and individually.

We have no need to go blindly along with Jim Jones or David Berg or David Koresh or any other self-declared spiritual leader. Rather, we are to follow the Spirit of truth, who will teach us all things (see John 14:17, 26). No lie can come from the truth, John declares (1 John 2:21). Only by knowing what is true, however, can we discern the lie.

The ages have witnessed many false christs and many self-proclaimed messiahs who have proved to be false and their words lies. We need to make sure that whatever the claims we encounter, we test them by the evidence that God has provided in His Word. For as Jesus said, the devil will attempt to deceive even God's very elect at the end.

This is why it's so important to follow John's advice: "Obey the Spirit's teaching." Why? "For his Spirit teaches you about everything, and what he teaches is true, not false" (verse 27, TEV; see also verses 20, 21).

The key to true Christian fellowship is knowing the truth as it really is. It is the only way to avoid being sidetracked and led astray by the devil's distractions and false doctrines. How do we know the truth? It is as the Holy Spirit guides us (and we follow) into all truth (see John 16:13).

Scripture even counsels us to test the Holy Spirit Himself, to make sure of the Spirit whom we are following. God is so committed to our freedom of thought and choice that He will not compel anyone; He wishes us to make sure for ourselves that we really are listening to the truth.

Con artists?

The idea of "just believe whatever you are told" is an extremely dangerous view and leaves us open to the suggestions of Satan himself. Having a "warm feeling" that something is true doesn't mean it is necessarily right.

In our neighborhood the authorities have warned us to watch out for con artists trying to enter houses. One poses as an antiques valuer. Another pretends to be a representative from the local municipal council. But they all have the same aim—to convince you to let them into your home.

One recent report concerns two con artists who work together. They pose as officials from the gas company, looking for suspected gas leaks. Sometimes they even have fake identity cards. Once inside, one keeps you talking while the other "checks your house for gas leaks." Of course, he is actually helping himself to your valuables!

Just because they seem plausible does not mean you should believe their message. Some neighbors have been foolish enough to believe such con artists, and have suffered as a result.

You always need to check out what you're being told. The same principle applies in evaluating biblical interpretation.

John tells us: "Be sure, then, to keep in your hearts the message you heard from the beginning. If you keep that message, then you will always live in union with the Son and the Father.

And this is what Christ himself promised to give us—eternal life" (1 John 2:24, 25, TEV).

The apostle is adamant here. He exhibits no doubt, indecision, or skepticism! Probably he is remembering all those statements he recorded in his Gospel of Jesus speaking of the gift of eternal life. The acid test of genuine Christianity is that it reflects the attitudes, beliefs, and content of the gospel brought by Jesus. If any "new light" contradicts Scripture, you can be sure that it is not light at all!

The day He comes

When John says "Yes, my children, remain in union with him, so that when he appears we may be full of courage and need not hide in shame from him on the Day he comes" (verse 28, TEV), the apostle can be thinking only of Jesus' own promise: "After I go and prepare a place for you, I will come back and take you to myself, so that you will be where I am" (John 14:3, TEV). The Christian's hope is the same as God's: to be together again, forever; to have the barrier of sin removed completely; to see Jesus face-to-face in all His glory. This is what the blessed hope accomplishes.

The Second Coming is the center of Adventist preaching and the heart of our message. This same Jesus who died to save and heal us will return to take us home. But why, then, are we so feeble in proclaiming our hope? Why doesn't it seem to affect us anymore? Have we heard it so often that it no longer makes any difference?

Let me ask a personal question: What does the Advent hope do for you? If it is only one of the doctrines or some agreed-upon part of belief that does not inspire and change you, then it is dead and useless in your life.

We need to *personalize* the blessed hope so that it *means* something to all of us. And it is not about the future at all. *It's about how we live here and now! Now* is the only time we have. And this is where we make our decisions—and all our decisions must be made in the light of the Second Coming.

What does a true awareness of Christ's second advent do for us? "Everyone who has this hope in Christ keeps himself pure, just as Christ is pure" (1 John 3:3, TEV). Taking His promise to return seriously means we live right by pleasing God, that we live close to Jesus daily.

At the same time we do not keep such an incredible promise to ourselves, but share and explain it to others. "Be ready at all times to answer anyone who asks you to explain the hope you have in you" (1 Peter 3:15, TEV). "Because we have this hope, we are very bold" (2 Cor. 3:12, TEV). We don't need to be ashamed or scared of telling others.

The Second Coming is not a cunning fable or human invention, but the very word of God. Having given us the glorious anticipation of the Advent, He will bring it about. He that cannot lie has promised. My prayer for you is this: "May the God of hope fill you with all joy and peace as you trust in him, so that you may overflow with hope by the power of the Holy Spirit" (Rom. 15:13).

I pray that the God of hope will give you this undying hope, and that it may soon be realized!

1 John 3:1-10

Children of God

6

The great flower-selling scam

One day when I was about 5 a woman came to our house selling small bouquets of flowers. My mother took out her purse and gave her sixpence (nowadays equivalent to about four cents!). For me that was a lot of money, so I started thinking how I could get into this lucrative business.

I set to work. Finding an old basket in the garage, I went out to the garden and picked all the best flowers I could find. Then I persuaded my younger sister that she should be the flower girl. (No way was I going to be a flower seller! Even at that early age I was rigid about gender roles.)

So off we went down the street. I told 3-year-old Jane what she was to say: "Hello, I've come to give you some flowers." And as soon as the woman of the house accepted, she was to be asked for payment. Cunning sales approach, I thought. Give 'em the flowers and then ask for cash. I'd go far . . .) My role was to supervise by hiding behind gateposts.

At the first house the woman looked a little surprised, but paid up. So did the next. I could hear cash registers ringing in my head. This was going well—money for a few dumb flowers.

At the third house disaster hit. The woman smiled politely at Jane and asked if her mommy knew she was out selling flowers. "No," Jane said in her wide-eyed innocence, then explained that it was all her brother's idea. The woman told Jane to wait there while she called our home.

My mother arrived like a whirling tornado. First she asked what

41

I thought I was doing. I explained, hoping to get points for initiative. No way. Mother was definitely upset.

   I had to go back to all the houses, repay the money, and apologize. "After all," Mother said, "if you're *giving,* then you don't ask to get *paid."* But even more than any of this was her shock at what people would think of all of us. "That's not the kind of family you belong to, my boy."

Slowly it sank into my thick skull that I had misrepresented our family. In my eagerness to make some quick money I was ready to exploit people (including my sister) and exchange my mother's flowers for some cash in my pockets (which would no doubt have been spent on candy and other junk).

Later that evening we had family talk time. I was asked if I didn't get pocket money anyway. Didn't I have everything I needed? And why had I used my sister and my mother's flowers and our neighbors' generosity just to make more money for myself?

Part of God's family

Through it all I saw why each member of a family is important—because we share not just a name, but a character and a reputation. So when it comes to being children of God, we too have to reflect the characteristics of God's family. Although we may take the name "Christian," unless we really are who we say we are, then we are just impostors exploiting the situation. That's why John is so clear: "Consider the incredible love that the Father has shown us in allowing us to be called 'children of God'—and that is not just what we are called, but what we *are"* (1 John 3:1, Phillips).

Not just what God calls us, but what He makes us! It is no formal declaration. What God is interested in is actually changing us into His true children.

True children

Think of all the characteristics of children—those fascinating, attractive traits. Truly "children are the most beautiful flowers of all" (Oscar Wilde). Maybe that's particularly why God wants to identify us as His children. For children are (or should be!) honest, truthful, direct, innocent, uncomplicated, ready to love without conditions, transparent, easily pleased, not devious, and most of all, *trusting.*

I believe it is this quality that God appreciates most of all, for if we truly trust Him, then He can really help and heal us. Without that trust (call it faith, if you like) God is unable to reveal His forgiveness, His transforming power, His salvation.

Many of these qualities vanish with adulthood. We learn to become suspicious, distrusting, deceptive even. But in the words of Carl Jung: "If there is anything that we wish to change in the child, we should first examine it and see whether it is not something that could better be changed in ourselves." Or as the ancient writer Mencius put it: "The great man is he who does not lose his child's heart."

We need to have our "child's heart" as we come to God. We do not approach Him with a faith that is blind, but one that looks as honestly and innocently as a child, who can see so clearly who can be trusted or not. Every one of us needs to return to that childlike way of seeing things. So how do you see spiritually? Do you behold the chariots of fire, or are your eyes still blinded? (see 2 Kings 6:17).

Such sight is truly the gift of God. "Yet to all who received him, to those who believed in his name, he gave the right to become children of God" (John 1:12; note also Rom. 8:18).

In contrast to this world, the children of God shine with the brilliance of God's truth: "So that you may become blameless and pure, children of God without fault in a crooked and depraved generation, in which you shine like stars in the universe" (Phil. 2:15).

How do we know whether we really are God's children, able to love one another? "This is how we know that we love the children of God: by loving God and carrying out his commands" (1 John 5:2).

The whole idea of being God's actual children should thrill and excite us. I remember speaking at my children's school. I decided to ask the young people to act out the story of the widow of Nain (Luke 7:11-17). One group was the funeral party, with the widow at the front mourning the loss of her only son. Those in it were crying and sad. And the kids played their parts well. On the other side of the room were Jesus, His disciples, and a crowd of happy people. When the two groups met, the silence that fell felt absolutely natural. Then with the raising of the young man, all the kids started rejoicing as if they had actually seen him come back from the dead!

That's the kind of happy thrill that should come from meeting

Jesus. Knowing that we are truly God's children should make us as happy as those unself-conscious schoolchildren.

Like God!

Now that we are God's children, we participate in all that He has planned. For "we know that when he appears, we shall be like him, for we shall see him as he is" (1 John 3:2). This most amazing statement depicts a profound miracle. As Peter puts it, we become "partakers of the divine nature" (2 Peter 1:4, KJV)! Paul echoes him: "We, who with unveiled faces all reflect the Lord's glory, are being transformed into his likeness with ever-increasing glory, which comes from the Lord" (2 Cor. 3:18).

It is an incredible concept! But if we are really God's children, then we shouldn't be surprised at what our loving heavenly Father has in store for us. It is the *likeness to God* that should thrill us about going to heaven, not the streets of gold or the angels' wings—not even living forever.

Significantly, God is just reverting to the way His universe really runs. We should not be surprised that He will destroy the false illusion that we call reality and replace it with "real reality"! For "we don't know what we shall become in the future. We only know that, *if reality were to break through,* we should reflect his likeness, for we should see him as he really is" (1 John 3:2, Phillips; my emphasis).

Seeing God as He really is—that's what John defines as the transforming event! We don't have to wait until the end to begin the process, either. As we seek out God and discover what He is really like—when we see Him as He actually is—then we will be changed and remade in His likeness. Even now I see many good friends of God who are truly His children in this way—persons who operate from the same principles as God and who try to reflect His ways to those around them.

No more sin

Of course, as John continues to say, God's children must reflect God's family, as I learned in my flower-selling scam. If you are truly a child of God, then sin is alien to you. God and sin can never go together. No longer can the child of God willingly and happily indulge in sin. "No one who is born of God will continue to sin" (verse 9).

The apostle meets head-on those who misunderstand God's promises of acceptance as license to sin. "He who does what is sinful is of the devil. . . . Anyone who does not do what is right is not a child of God; nor is anyone who does not love his brother" (verses 8-10). All too many Christians have fallen into the trap of thinking that because God is forgiveness personified, then it doesn't really matter what you do or how you live. Some have even argued that it makes God's graciousness that much greater—the "happy sin" that leads God to demonstrate His wonderful goodness.

Paul also strongly counters such a dangerous error. "Shall we sin to our heart's content and see how far we can exploit the grace of God? What a ghastly thought!" (Rom. 6:1, 2, Phillips). (Note that neither Paul nor John is speaking about the sins of accident and circumstance, but rather the premeditated and deliberate attitude that exploits and takes advantage of God's grace. Such presumption on God's forgiving nature can lead only to a carelessness that denies sin's fatal nature.)

On the other hand, we must see sin not just as the breaking of rules. The fact that we may keep the legal requirements does not make us good. My mother used to make wonderful chocolate cakes and then set them out on the windowsill to cool. I always received strict instructions not to touch them. But I would examine the cake, see if maybe a crumb had fallen off, and look at ways of cutting a piece without my mother knowing. But of course, I could never work out how to do it without getting caught. So when Mother told me I was a good boy for not touching the cake, I had to own up and explain that if I could've taken a piece, I would have!

God wants to take us to a higher level than mere technical obedience. He longs to explain to each one of us, much as my mother did, that it was for my best, and didn't I know we were going to have cake for tea anyway? God seeks our willing agreement that His way is inherently and intrinsically right and true. He longs for us to say with Him that right really is right, not just because He tells us it is. In the words of Rabindranath Tagore, "God seeks comrades and claims love, the devil seeks slaves and claims obedience."

Dealing with lawlessness

The spirit God has to deal with is not just one of rule-breaking. It is the attitude to God and the law that lies behind all of this—a spirit that is anti-law in the same way that the devil is anti-Christ. John makes it clear when he says: "Sin is lawlessness" (1 John 3:4). It is a whole way of living, not just an occasional breaking of the regulations. Sin is a complete rejection of God as the source of the way, the truth, and the life. And it is a determined decision to live a life in rebellion, seeking your own way, which, as God so clearly states, leads to destruction.

The reason God has to remove sin from us is not so much because of a reaction of "holy horror" on His part. Rather, it is because He knows that sin kills and that if we cling to our sinfulness, then we will die. It's as simple as that, and God does not want to lose any of His children. Ultimately He gives us all the freedom of choice, but not before making the need for the decision as clear as He can. If even then we choose to reject His love, His healing, His salvation, He will allow it. We find no "universal salvation" here—God is so committed to our freedom that He will never force us to come to Him. But as we reap what we have sown, God will not rejoice. Instead, He will weep over the loss of His beloved yet rebellious children.

God wishes more than anything else to be the one who takes away our sinfulness. That is the reason Jesus came. "He appeared so that he might take away our sins" (verse 5). On the cross Jesus, who was made to be sin although He knew no sin (2 Cor. 5:21), became our healing, life-giving Saviour. We no longer have to live with the guilt and pain of our sinful actions (Micah 7:19) because God creates us anew. So why should we ever want to go back to a life of sin? But if sin remains dominant in our lifestyle, then the words of John condemn us: "No one who continues to sin has either seen him or known him" (1 John 3:6). The apostle's plea is not a threat, but an appeal to come to Jesus and receive His healing salvation before it is too late.

Just as those around Him did not recognize Jesus for what He really was, we should not be surprised if the world does not know us either. If they do not know God, the ways of a Christian seem absurd to them. "The reason the world does not know us is that it did not know him" (verse 1). In this John echoes the words of Jesus he recorded in his Gospel: "If the world hates you, keep in mind that it hated me first. If you belonged to the world, it would love you as its own. As it is, you do not belong to the world, but I have chosen you out of the world. That is why the world hates you" (John 15:18, 19).

You cannot have it both ways! Either you choose God or you reject Him. We all are very much aware of sin in our individual lives. We must avoid the belief that we can be saved *in* sin rather than saved *from* sin and must always remember that sin is horrifying and destructive—a sign that God's grace must be sought again and again.

The true son or daughter of God must let the Spirit exterminate the attitude of lawlessness, the very character of the antichrist, from his or her life. This cannot happen through human effort, for it's God's work alone. "The reason the Son of God appeared was to destroy the devil's work" (1 John 3:8). Our part now is to live as true children of God who follow and agree with our Father's ways.

Love One Another

7

The wedding symbol

Everybody loves a wedding. Is it the service, the bride in white, the reception? Or is it because a wedding illustrates the ideal of love and hope and commitment? However doubtful the marriage may seem, whatever misgivings others may have, the promises made in the ceremony rise above all such concerns. Why? Because we *want* the marriage to be happy and successful, we want to believe in endless love and eternal commitment, even though the evidence of some marriages points the other way!

The wedding is the great love symbol. As we watch the exchange of vows, as bride and groom gaze into each other's eyes, as they kiss, we smile. We long for them to be in love forever, to find total and complete happiness in each other—because we desire the same for ourselves. And while we may always fall short of the ideal, we stretch out for it in hope.

As a symbol of love commitment the wedding also represents the ideal relationship with God. The promises made between man and woman before God illustrate the promises we want to share with Him. Scripture uses the close and intimate marriage relationship to depict the closeness and intimacy we need to have with God (see, for example, 1 Cor. 6:17; Rev. 21).

If you're married, reflect on your own wedding. What are your memories? Some humorous perhaps, some anxious moments, but hopefully a wonderful, beautiful day—whatever has happened since. If you're not married, what about all the weddings you've been to? What were they to you? Even if tragedies and divorces followed afterward—even if you yourself are divorced—this does not change the beauty of the wedding, its taste of heaven on earth.

For this is the heart of John's thought: "This is the message you heard from the beginning: We should love one another" (1 John 3:11).

A story tells of the apostle John in his old age when he was so infirm that he had to have someone carry him everywhere. As he was brought into the church at Ephesus, all he did was repeat, "Little children, love one another." When someone asked him why he kept repeating just this one command, he said, "Because it is enough."

While this story may or may not be historically correct, its intent is true. True, that is, when understood in the context of real Christian love, rather than some kind of vague "warm feeling of attraction," the normal use of the word *love* today.

What's love got to do with it?

"What's love got to do with it?" a member once asked me. For him, the God-human relationship rested not on love, but on fulfilling requirements. It is somewhat like the difference between the love relationship of a marriage and the marriage certificate. One is relational; the other is legal. To stress the legal aspect does not make the marriage work. In fact, to descend to legal requirements usually means the marriage is virtually over. When the lawyers move in and everything is down to contracts, then where is love? After all, if I go to my wife waving our marriage certificate in her face and demanding that she fulfill her obligations, how is she likely to respond?

Just as a marriage cannot be forced to work by observing legal requirements, our relationship to God cannot be governed by the law. For while the law is real and important, love is the fulfilling of the law.

Unfortunately, we hear a lot of nonsense about love. For example, that it's a "secondhand emotion." It means not having to say you're sorry. Love is blind. And all of that nice-sounding slush that has very little to do with the God of love.

How do we sort out the true from the false? Check out the following definitions of love:

49

THE ULTIMATE GOD

Love is:

"A sickness full of woes" (Samuel Daniel).
"Desperate madness" (John Ford).
"Sentimental measles" (Charles Kingsley).
"A kind of warfare" (Ovid).
"A grave mental disease" (Plato).
"A mutual misunderstanding" (Oscar Wilde).
"The drug which makes sexuality palatable in popular mythology" (Germaine Greer).
"Sex to the last" (John Dryden).
"Yesterday's illusion, today's allusion, and tomorrow's delusion" (Warren Goldberg).
"A game in which both players always cheat" (Edgar W. Howe).

How much do you understand about love from that list? That love is madness, a sickness, a sexual drug? That love is an illusion, a kind of cheating game, or at best just a total misunderstanding? How degraded is the view of love that most believe in! But that's the way so many live their lives, with love as some dreamlike feeling.

Yet the reality is so different! Note these definitions from a Christian perspective:

"Love is service rather than sentiment" (John R. W. Stott).
"Love does not say, 'Give me,' but 'Let me give you'" (Jill Briscoe).
"Love must love even when it gets nothing out of it" (Roger Forster).
"Love is practical, or it is not love at all" (P. W. Howard).
"Christian love is not the victim of our emotions, but the servant of our will" (John R. W. Stott).
"Love is not blind. Lust is blind. If love is blind, God is blind" (Gordon Palmer).
"Nobody will know what you mean by saying 'God is love' unless you act it as well" (Lawrence Pearsall Jacks).

John himself has much to say about such divine love in his Epistles: "But if anyone obeys his word, God's love is truly made

50

complete in him. This is how we know we are in him" (1 John 2:5).

"This is how we know what love is: Jesus Christ laid down his life for us. And we ought to lay down our lives for our brothers" (1 John 3:16).

"No one has ever seen God; but if we love one another, God lives in us and his love is made complete in us" (1 John 4:12).

"In this way, love is made complete among us so that we will have confidence on the day of judgment, because in this world we are like him" (verse 17).

The God who is love

Through our ability to love we most clearly reflect the image of God. And because God is love, He made us—for love wishes to have someone to love, someone to relate to. God made us to love and be loved, and when anything hurts or destroys that capacity, then we are that much less like God. This is why your ability to love and be loved is under so much attack, for the evil one knows that that is the best way to pervert and misrepresent the God who is love.

So how does John explain how we know what love is? He spells it out for all those who might want to confuse the issue: "This is how we know what love is: Jesus Christ laid down his life for us." Just that—and as simple as that! And what is the consequence? "And we ought to lay down our lives for our brothers" (1 John 3:16).

For those who look down on other Christians as second-class citizens of the kingdom, this is the ultimate rebuke. John tells those "gnostics" who thought they were a spiritual elite, who thought themselves so much better than the rest, that what really matters is their willingness to die for those they look down on!

The apostle is definite here. Again and again he makes plain his conviction that we are to love in actions, not just words (verse 18). Love certainly is more than talk, as Jesus made so clear on the cross.

The trouble with Cain

John uses the illustration of Cain to make his point. "We must not be like Cain; he belonged to the Evil One and murdered his own brother Abel. Why did Cain murder him? Because the things he himself did were wrong, and the things his brother did were right" (verse 12, TEV).

Cain, a farmer, decided he would give a gift of his produce to God. Although he knew that it was not what God had asked for, he, like so many today, thought he knew better than God. But his "offering" destroyed the symbolism that God wanted to make so clear—that sin results in death. The sacrifice of Jesus that God intended to be demonstrated in the sacrificial system obviously could not be seen in Cain's offerings of farm produce. You can even detect in Cain's actions a self-reliant attitude, a self-righteousness, and a reliance on works righteousness.

This is why Scripture records that the Lord "rejected Cain and his offering. Cain became furious, and he scowled in anger. Then the Lord said to Cain, 'Why are you angry? Why that scowl on your face? If you had done the right thing, you would be smiling; but because you have done evil, sin is crouching at your door. It wants to rule you, but you must overcome it'" (Gen. 4:5-7, TEV).

From the account it's clear that Cain knew exactly what he was doing and that his attitude to God was one of rebellion and defiance. As a result, God had to spell out graphically that the very essence of sin is to reject Him and go your own way. Cain's rejection of God led quickly to sin's inherent results—violence and murder!

John adds to this clear depiction of evil the chilling statement that "whoever hates his brother is a murderer" (1 John 3:15, TEV). In other words, if we refuse to follow God's way and thus love one another, we are in the same league as Cain. That frightening idea should give us all pause for thought.

Reconciliation

My friend Fred tells this story to illustrate what can happen when we adopt the "ministry of reconciliation" (2 Cor. 5:18, KJV).

Fred was working on an old man's house. He thought that the man was certainly past 90. As they were talking one day, the old man said, "Don't look around now. My brother is going past, and I don't speak to him. In fact, I haven't spoken to him for 40 years."

Astounded, Fred suggested that since both men were late in life ("you both have one foot in the grave," as he rather directly put it!), it was time for them to make up. Perhaps he could speak to his brother or write him a letter.

"Well," said the man, "if my brother wishes to speak to me or write to me, I would accept that. But I'm not going to be the first to act."

Fred suggested he consider beginning the process himself.

A couple days later Fred was sitting in a café when the old man appeared and told him he had taken the advice. "In fact, I can't stop to talk to you; I'm off to see my brother right now." Fred wished him well and told him he'd be praying for them both.

Later Fred learned that the two old brothers had met and spoken to each other for the first time in 40 years. They could not even remember the reason they had fallen out with each other so many years ago!

And within a couple months they both died. How tragic that 40 years had been wasted, 40 years that they could have spent in brotherly love! But at least before death they had become reconciled.

How much more we need to share our ministry of reconciliation, for it is an active demonstration of the way "God was in Christ, reconciling the world unto himself" (verse 19, KJV).

God's love is the answer to the barriers that sin raises between people and especially between people and God—"Who shall separate us from the love of Christ?" (Rom. 8:35). Jesus' ministry is God making it possible for us to come back to Him. He is the connection, the link, the bridge, the ladder, the way across the gulf sin has created.

How? Because Jesus Himself is God. "Anyone who has seen me has seen the Father" (John 14:9). "I and the Father are one" (John 10:30). God provides the way across that infinite gulf—He Himself is the way. For "while we were yet sinners, Christ died for us" (Rom. 5:8, KJV).

Have you ever had a fight? Have you ever become angry with someone? A family quarrel, perhaps? A long-standing feud?

We all get mad with someone sometime—and the bitterness may be great. Yet once it is over and gone, and the flash of anger has disappeared, then the process of getting back together must begin. It may take a long time, but a tremendous sense of love returns with a true reconciliation—the relationship is restored.

So it is with us and God. We are the party in the wrong—the guilty, the sinful, the evil-natured ones. Yet because of His immeasurable goodness and love, and because He knows we can't help ourselves, God takes the initiative and makes it possible for us to be with Him again.

Who does it all? God—not we ourselves, not anybody else, but God. Read, in 2 Corinthians 5:18, 19; Hebrews 2:17; and Colossians 1:19-22, how He does this.

But what does this reconciliation mean? Where do you go after being reconciled? After a dispute and then reconciliation, do people just say goodbye and leave it at that? Reconciliation implies a future process—a using of the reconciliation to make something more, something even greater. John makes clear we need to put our reconciliation into action: "If anyone has material possessions and sees his brother in need, but has no pity on him, how can the love of God be in him?" (1 John 3:17). We must take direct personal action and make sure our love for our fellow human beings reflects God's love for us.

From death to life!

"We know that we have passed from death to life, because we love our brothers. Anyone who does not love remains in death" (verse 14).

Strange, isn't it, how we can know something, yet refuse to allow that fact to affect our lives? Perhaps we can agree that something is right, yet decline to do it. Or we can accept that a certain course of action will help us, yet not follow it.

We need to accept the truth that in Christ we have truly passed from death to life! And the proof of that fact is in the spirit of love we demonstrate to "our brothers"—those around us. Only if we love one another do we reveal that we truly love God, and have eternal life.

1 John 4:1-6

Spirit-testing

8

Spiritual sense

Evelyn Glennie is one of the world's best-known percussionists. From xylophones to glockenspiels to snare drums to cymbals, she is a multitalented virtuoso. She plays more than 200 instruments, and is always experimenting with more. Besides the fact that she has the most amazing musical ability, there's one thing more you should know about Evelyn Glennie.

She is totally deaf.

Watching a TV documentary about this brilliant musician, I wondered how she did it. How could you be so sharp and expressive, and yet not be able to hear what you were playing?

She explained how. A music teacher at school had made her place her hands against the wall, and then asked which of the two drums struck made which sound. Sure enough, Evelyn could tell them apart because the vibrations she felt on the wall made different patterns on her hands. The young woman could literally feel the sounds.

Developing this ability, she found she could describe what each instrument "felt" like in the vibrations her body detects. Deep round vibrations swell out from the low notes. High notes make sharp and brief vibrations, and so on. And using language that sounds strange to those of us who hear, she describes the "vibration shape" of each instrument.

If you or I had been Evelyn Glennie, what would we have done if someone had encouraged us to try music? Would we have said that with such a disability music was a pointless exercise? Probably. But by developing and extending a sense that most of us ignore, Glennie has become an example of how much can be done in music, even if you are deaf.

So what of the spiritual world? We may say we cannot see spiritually. But in the same way that physical senses can be developed, we can train our spiritual sensitivity. Only by repeated practice can we grow spiritually, but grow we must.

Test the spirits

We are spiritually gullible if we believe whatever we're told. Just because someone *claims* to be speaking for God does not make it true. "My dear friends, do not believe all who claim to have the Spirit, but test them to find out if the spirit they have comes from God. For many false prophets have gone out everywhere" (1 John 4:1, TEV).

Here John is dealing with those who were promoting the idea that Jesus was not truly a human being. Such individuals taught that Jesus was an "emanation" of God or some kind of ghost—a being who only "seemed" to take on human form. But John knew that to deny the humanity of Jesus was to strike at the root of the gospel. Jesus came as one of us, to live among us and to die at our hands— to show us truly who God really is. He did not use His divinity for His own advantage, but depended upon His heavenly Father, as we must too. More than this, to deny Christ's humanity is to deny that He was tempted in all points like as we are, yet without sin (see Heb. 4:15).

As we discuss the nature of Christ we need to combat the extremes some go to. Here John deals with those who deny the humanity of Christ. In his Gospel, especially in the first chapter, he refutes those who reject the divinity of Christ. Both errors destroy the gospel message of Jesus as fully God and fully man, who reveals in human form the character of God.

The problem is not really with those who attack the church from the outside. The real danger comes from those within who claim that they have the Spirit of God.

John has just said that "because of the Spirit that God has given us we know that God lives in union with us" (1 John 3:24, TEV). But dissident groups inside the church were offering this same claim! So now John tackles this problem, making it clear that those who disagree with the historic message of Jesus cannot have the Spirit of God. If they deny that Jesus came "in the flesh," they are wrong. They are also wrong if they dispute any truth already preached. "We are from God, and whoever knows God listens to us; but whoever is not from God does not listen to us. This is how we recognize the Spirit of truth and the spirit of falsehood" (1 John 4:6).

False prophets

Many false prophets weave much truth into their system of error. Some sound extremely pious and act with great religious zeal. They can be extremely convincing when they claim, "I have just received this message from God Himself." But John says that even if they sound believable and seem to be righteous, "test the spirits"!

I remember a colleague from the time I worked in industry who confided in me one day that he had special revelations. I invited Martin to our house to explain, and he arrived together with a number of "disciples," all young women. He began from a seemingly Christian viewpoint, but as we talked, it became clear that he was mixing in Eastern mysticism, too. Martin spoke of the "eye of faith" that one needed in discovering truth, and said that only those who discovered this "eye of faith" (under his direction!) could achieve salvation. In many ways Martin paralleled the mind-set of those whom John was dealing with. My friend and his followers spoke of "special knowledge" and "secret revelations." As the evening wore on, Martin's ideas deviated from the Bible more and more. I kept calling their attention back to biblical truth and the need for "testing the spirits" "by the law and by the testimony," "by their fruits," and so on.

The conversation began to become quite heated; then suddenly one of the girls burst out with a curse against the Bible. They did not want to hear their leader contradicted by the Bible, and so would rather damn Scripture than give up their belief in their guru.

At that, the situation became totally clear to me. Anyone who curses Scripture cannot have the truth, and I told them so. They soon left, even though I wanted to share more of the truth I knew. But those who have rejected the Bible as the source of truth about God are hard to help. "Every spirit that does not acknowledge Jesus is not from God" (verse 3).

Foolish?

We are truly foolish if we accept as genuine any claim without first carefully investigating it. If we would not do this in the material world, why then should we ignore God's gift of mental ability when it comes to examining matters in the spiritual realm?

Sometimes certain individuals will argue that it is "rationalism" to wish to look at the evidence and test the validity of what someone puts forward as "divine truth." They may suggest that we should be "convicted" by the "warm feeling" that the truth is supposed to bring. Again the trouble is that there are any number of religious beliefs that people claim give them such "warm feelings."

God does not wish us to base our belief and trust in Him on feelings, even though we must not leave our emotional reaction out of our faith. He encourages us to "taste and see that the Lord is good" (Ps. 34:8, KJV)—to experiment and examine for ourselves the truth that He wishes us to accept.

Scripture tells us to test God's will—in fact, to test everything. "Do not conform any longer to the pattern of this world, but be transformed by the renewing of your mind. Then you will be able to test and approve what God's will is—his good, pleasing and perfect will" (Rom. 12:2).

"Test everything. Hold on to the good" (1 Thess. 5:21).

The Bible also instructs us to carefully search ourselves—not to rely on what we may or may not feel, but to study the evidence of Christian belief in our own lives. "Examine yourselves to see whether you are in the faith; test yourselves. Do you not realize that Christ Jesus is in you—unless, of course, you fail the test?" (2 Cor. 13:5).

"Each one should test his own actions. Then he can take pride in himself, without comparing himself to somebody else" (Gal. 6:4).

Like the Scripture searchers of Berea, who checked out what Paul had to say by comparing it with the Old Testament to make sure what he was presenting was true (Acts 17:10, 11), we need to know the Bible so well that we can determine whether any statement is in agreement with it or not. We need to be Bible-based believers!

Science

The true principles of science apply just as much in the way we approach spiritual truth as any other kind of truth. While pursuing my chemistry degree I learned much about the scientific method and how, when properly applied, it leads to a deeper understanding of what is really true. First you examine the available evidence. You do not come with a biased mind, but one eager to discover what is true. Perhaps then you come up with a theory that fits the facts before you—a hypothesis, if you like. Next you devise some kind of test or experiment that will aid you in determining whether your theory might be correct or not.

Take our experiments with nitrogen triiodide.

Now, as budding chemists we had read of the substance. We even had some idea about how it should be made, which I will not reveal here, for reasons that will become obvious.

Our examination of the written evidence led us to believe that this chemical compound might be very unstable, for it consisted of two very different elements normally existing independently. So we had our theory. Now we needed to test it.

Mixing various chemical solutions, we produced a purplish precipitate that we could filter off. While it was still wet, it was fine, but our theory was proved absolutely true when it dried up.

I still remember that exciting moment when we touched a small sample of the purple powder. With a crackling bang it disappeared, and where there had once been powder there was now a purple cloud!

We had proved our theory true. And we continued our "tests" of this purple substance by coating doorknobs and desktops with a wet paste of nitrogen triiodide. I leave it to your imagination what the result was when the chemistry lecturer opened the door and went over to his desk . . .

When it comes to the Bible, we are to compare scripture with scripture; we are to use our minds, guided by the Holy Spirit; we are to make sure we know *why* we believe. We need to *evaluate* the evidence and *test* the claims.

The end

As the end of the world approaches, the great deceiver will present miraculous signs and wonders as "evidence" for his claims. If we have allowed marvels and the supposedly supernatural to sway our minds, we will be deluded. Anyone who makes such miracles and apparent manifestations of the "Spirit" a test of faith will discover that Satan's ability to counterfeit will lead us to accept him as a plausible "angel of light." Inspiration warns us against believing the claims of human beings and the miracles of even supposed angels. Especially when it comes to an angelic representation of "another gospel"—another "version" of the truth—we should be alert to the alarm signal: "But even if we or an angel from heaven should preach a gospel other than the one we preached to you, let him be eternally condemned" (Gal. 1:8).

It is a real tragedy how many apparently sensible and rational people are more than ready to swallow false gospels. Paganism is alive and well, and is being reborn often in a Christian disguise. The counsel to "test the spirits" is more important than ever!

And it is not just in the non-Christian world. Attending a recent Christian Booksellers' Convention here in the United Kingdom, I asked one Christian publisher what people were buying these days. I had hoped the answer would be that they were purchasing the Bible and good Bible-based books with deep spiritual insights. But his answer really shocked me. "What Christians are looking for is the spectacular, miraculous, fascinating, spellbinding. Feelings and amazing experiences are the thing."

John's advice is nothing new. Remember how God counseled ancient Israel that even if the "prophet" accurately forecasts the future but tries to lead you away from God, then do not follow (see Deut. 13:1-3).

The sad fact is that this is what so many people, even in the religious world, do actually want. They want the signs and wonders, and almost *demand* them. But remember the words of Jesus in response to such demands? "Then some of the Pharisees and teachers of the law said to him, 'Teacher, we want to see a miraculous sign from you.' He answered, 'A wicked and adulterous generation asks for a miraculous sign! But none will be given it except the sign of the prophet Jonah'" (Matt. 12:38, 39; see also 1 Cor. 1:22).

The false religions of the modern world fool people by appealing to their desire for the bizarre and the extraordinary. They confuse and amaze and deceive all at once, and when you suggest that you might want to investigate their validity, such people respond, "Don't ask questions! You must take it all on faith!"

But this is not biblical faith. For how does God act? Consider what Jesus did on the road to Emmaus. He did not overwhelm the two disciples by divine authority or by amazing signs, but convinced them by *appealing to the truth of Scripture* (see Luke 24:13ff.). Remember the warnings about false christs and counterfeit miracles (see Matt. 24:24, 25 and 2 Thess. 2:9, 10)?

The important question for us always to consider is not how good are the fireworks and the wonder, but *is it true?*

We resist deception, not by our own strength and power, but by having God and His truth. "You, dear children, are from God and have overcome them, because the one who is in you is greater than the one who is in the world" (1 John 4:4).

In our lives we are to reveal that Jesus—fully divine, fully human—is the source and objective of our beliefs. Only then will we be proving that we are of the right Spirit, only then will we have authority to speak the truth, and only then will Jesus truly "live in us." In this way we and others will be able to recognize the Spirit of God (see verse 6).

A Christian friend of mine was intrigued about the beliefs of spiritualists. One day he went to a service at a spiritualist church where the subject advertised was "Are the Dead Alive?" The presenter claimed that he would provide absolute proof. Remembering what the Bible says about the state of the dead, my friend became a little nervous and wondered whether he should stay.

Then as they stood for the opening hymn, he noticed that the piano was playing by itself. That was enough for him! He left, and didn't stop to find out whether it was just a hoax or whether some "spirit" was actually playing.

Knowing what the Bible says about such subjects should be enough for us not to put ourselves in such situations. If we cannot recognize the spirit of falsehood, then we are wide open to deception. Test the spirits!

How God Is Love

9

Does not compute

I picked up my portable computer, ready to get busy. I smiled to myself because I felt as though I was really getting organized. Using today's high-tech tools, I was at the cutting edge of what's happening in our modern world. Now for some serious high-profile research in the library. *Look at all those poor people still working with pen and paper,* I thought to myself.

Then I noticed something and choked off a scream just before it hit my vocal cords. *I'd forgotten the power cord!* How could I have done that? How frustratingly foolish can you get? I stared at the useless piece of equipment sitting dead and lifeless in front of me. Looking around, wondering who might be watching me and noticing my stupidity, I closed up the computer and put it back into its case, trying to appear nonchalant and unconcerned.

Inside I was angry and upset. How *could* I have done that? Moron, imbecile, dimwit, half-brained amoeba (I can think of many insults for myself!). Bringing a computer without a power cord! That's about as useful as a car with an empty fuel tank or a flashlight with no batteries. I had no power!

Our world, so full of wonderful inventions, lacks spiritual power. Many say they belong to God and claim His empowering Spirit, but eventually deny the Spirit's power (see 2 Tim. 3:5). And I, despite all my theological training and church experience, am dead and lifeless without the power of God.

So it was back to basics. Even without my technological wonders and my computer wizardry, I could still work. I smiled back at one puzzled student as I put my computer down beside me. Laughing at my own foolishness, I picked up my pen.

The power of love

The power of God is His incredible love. God and love appear together in 14 of the verses of 1 John! I believe this tells us that John's message stems from his own personal experience of standing at the foot of the cross and looking up into the eyes of his dying Saviour. Of all the disciples, he was the only one there. Only the brave women were there with him!

But as John saw Jesus demonstrate the love of God in the agony of crucifixion, as Christ took upon Himself the results of sin, as He died the sinner's death, the apostle realized what love really means, how salvation is accomplished, and how we are reconciled to God. John recognized that "this is how God showed his love among us: He sent his one and only Son into the world that we might live through him" (1 John 4:9).

At one

The atonement is the heart of the gospel. Unfortunately, the very word "atonement" in modern English can perhaps convey something other than the original intention. When we "atone" for something today, we generally mean that we are trying to make amends, to placate anger or soothe hostility.

When I arrive late for work, my boss is upset and annoyed. I "atone" for my violation of office rules by promising to stay an extra hour in the evening. Such ideas of "atoning"—paying off an offense—are a far cry from the original meaning, which was exactly as the word says: of becoming, making, or being *at one*.

Christ's atonement, then, is the "one-ing" of us back to God, or in better grammatical English, making us as one, bringing us back into harmony, restoring unity and creating a union. All reflect the idea of removing separation and bringing two individuals together.

Traditional theories of the atonement are unsatisfactory in some ways because they do not capture the reality of what Christ has done. Most are concerned with *legality*—how a righteous God can legally forgive and pardon sinners. Note that they are theories, for the Bible does not give us a carefully and completely defined theory of the atonement. Rather, Scripture simply tells us it has happened!

But the perspective of the great controversy provides us a special insight into what the atonement means and how God accomplished it. The real question is What went wrong? If we can understand the problems that sin caused in God's universe, then we can see in the atonement God's wonderful solution.

Though Satan called God's law and government into question, the real argument was over the relationship between God and His created children. Was God trustworthy and loving, as He said? Was God righteous and truthful or a cruel tyrant? How could created beings determine one way or the other?

When Adam and Eve sinned, the sin was more than the breaking of certain rules; it was the shattering of their intimate relationship with their Creator and Father. In making the atonement, then, Jesus is not just working through the legal obligations, but seeking to restore the loving, trusting relationship that sin destroyed. Remember that, as the Bible makes clear, it is not something in God that needs changing—it is we who need to be changed! God was in Christ reconciling the world to Himself. Nowhere does Scripture suggest that God needed to be reconciled to us. The offense, the problem, is not in God, but in us as rebellious sinners.

Nor is the sacrifice of Jesus the means by which God is appeased and persuaded to love us once again. On the contrary, it was, as John says, because of the love of God that Christ came to be our salvation: "This is what love is: it is not that we have loved God, but that he loved us and sent his Son to be the means by which our sins are forgiven" (verse 10, TEV).

Divine love needed to be spelled out. As he looked back over his life, Paul described this patient, kind, unenvying, humble love in 1 Corinthians 13:4-7. It is a wonderful description of the love that comes from God that so rarely finds an echo in the way we love. On the contrary, human love is all too often the exact opposite: impatient, unkind, envious, boasting, proud, rude, self-seeking, angry. This kind of "love" does keep a record of wrongs, takes a perverse delight in evil, and hates truth.

Our human nature would like in some way to take the credit for some part of our salvation. Some even suggest that it is a kind of partnership: we love God, and He loves us, and that's the way we are saved. The idea that we come to God of ourselves and give Him our love so that He can then love and save us is the very opposite of the truth.

Let us not make ourselves out to be quite good people just needing a little fixing up. Let us instead put ourselves into the hands of our loving Divine Physician and allow Him to cure us of all our sin diseases.

The meaning of "God is love"

First John 4:7-21 is surely the most powerful passage in the Epistle. Here is the clear and direct declaration that *God is love,* and what such a declaration means to the Christian.

John defines love not as some vague feeling of attraction or physical infatuation, but, on God's part, as power, involving intellectual and moral strength. Rather than some kind of occasional impulse, divine love is constant, a principle based on the very character of God Himself. This living principle is ours only as we have a connection with God, a true relationship with Him. As Jesus summed up the law, the very essence of our beliefs is love to God and love to our fellow human beings.

To truly know God is to love Him. The devil may intellectually "know" God, but he does not wish to have a deep and intimate and loving relationship with Him. As John says: "Whoever loves is a child of God and knows God" (verse 7, TEV).

Those John is writing to believed that all that they needed was a special knowledge of God, some "secrets of salvation." They also saw themselves as the "special ones," and so excluded other Christians who did not have their particular knowledge. Consequently they had no place in their religious scheme for love for others outside their special group. This is absolutely wrong, John says. "Whoever does not love does not know God, for God is love" (verse 8, TEV). To interpret a little here, John is essentially saying, "You may claim a special knowledge of God. You think that you will be saved by what you know. But this knowledge of yours is not helping you at all. For if you really did have a true knowledge of God, you would recognize that God is love and that you must show this same kind of love to others."

Lest we see our love for God as something that earns us salvation, John quickly points out love's true nature: "This is what love is: it is not that we have loved God, but that he loved us and sent his Son to be the means by which our sins are forgiven" (verse 10, TEV).

Our love for God results from God's love for us. It is the *response* to God's salvation, not the cause. As we accept this divine love, this principle of power, it changes our characters, controls our passions, forgives our sins, and heals us of our sin-sickness. We can never achieve this by *trying* to love one another. All the attempts in the world will not work unless we have love for God and allow Him to work in us, to will and to do what we cannot do (see Phil. 2:13). In fact, when we are connected to God through love, then love comes from us spontaneously.

That is why we can love one another as Christians—because each of us has a common relationship to God. We are all part of the same family and love each other as God has already loved us (see 1 John 4:11).

Remember that love does not keep an account of wrongs, nor is it proud and selfish. Rather, "if we love one another, God lives in union with us, and his love is made perfect in us" (verse 12, TEV).

God's love is made perfect in us. We are the arena in which God reveals His love in the highest way, where He shows Himself to be truly the God of love. And if God manifests His love in us, then what should happen?

John answers the question for us: "Love is made perfect in us in order that we may have courage on the Judgment Day; and we will have it because our life in this world is the same as Christ's" (verse 17, TEV).

Love and fear

Are you fearful of the judgment? Does the thought of facing the end of the world fill you with terror? While we are not to dwell on the judgment before it happens, we do need to be sure, not of ourselves, but of where we are with God. We have assurance, as John says, because our life mirrors that of Christ. Only as we become more like Christ can we face the future. And that means Christlike love must be ours. Why?

Because "there is no fear in love; perfect love drives out all fear" (verse 18, TEV). We often read that text to mean that if *we* had perfect love, then we would not be fearful. But in the context John is speaking about *God's* perfect love. God's love, when received, makes it possible to live without fear.

A while ago I wrote a book about fear and how God ends our fear through His perfect love for us. This book has been translated into Russian, and a number of people from that tortured country have expressed their appreciation for it. But the most moving testimony to the wonderful gift of love that ends fear came from the former Yugoslavia. There a girl in the war zone read the book and found peace and comfort in the God who ends our fears. Only God's perfect love, demonstrated at Calvary, can end our fears.

Perhaps our greatest fears have been about God and what He will do to us unless we submit to Him. The first person anyone ever feared on earth was God Himself. Remember that Adam and Eve, after they had broken their relationship of trust, hid from Him. Adam even admitted he was afraid of God (see Gen. 3:10). But as John goes on to say, "Perfect love drives out fear, because fear has to do with punishment. The one who fears is not made perfect in love" (1 John 4:18).

How can you love someone you fear? I well remember one young woman who had been brought up to truly *fear* God telling me, "I know that God will get me in the end, but I could never love such a tyrant."

No, the truth is that if we are afraid of God, we cannot love Him. Most of our fear comes from misunderstandings about the judgment. If it is true that God deliberately tortures people to punish them for their evil at the end, then how can you possibly love Him? We must not avoid the terrible fact of the end-time destruction of the wicked; the fire that consumes them is totally real. But it is the glory of Him who is love that destroys, not a punitive, vengeful pagan deity. God allows all of us free choice; we all reap what we have sown, and the inherent self-destruction that is sin will finally come to all who have not accepted God's healing salvation. But fear of hell cannot force anyone to love God. Rather, only through seeing God as He truly is and responding to Him can we have a fearless future. "We love because he first loved us" (verse 19).

Love: power to change

When an electric current passes through a wire, we say the wire is "live." Electricity is power. When used as a source of energy, it can give heat and light, and power all types of machinery and equipment. You turn the switch, and the radio is *on;* it's "alive." Electricity hisses, crackles, and speaks—just as if it were a living thing. You fit a battery to a child's toy, and it moves across the floor just as if it were some live animal. It has power to become "alive."

"Christ in you, the hope of glory" (Col. 1:27) is the power of the God of love to save. Christ living in you is God's electricity to make you truly alive and able to live for Him. "For to me to live is Christ" (Phil. 1:21, KJV) is the connection with the source of this divine energy. Disconnection is death—turned off, unable to function, worse than useless.

For without the power of God we are all cut off, beings who have no way of working on our own. Without the power of Jesus living in us we are nothing. But with Jesus we are new creatures, working with Him and in Him because He is the source of power. Through Jesus, we "are being transformed into his likeness with ever-increasing glory" (2 Cor. 3:18).

This is what Jesus does for us and in us. He prepares us for an eternity with Him, transforming our sinful, fallen nature into a glorious nature, the nature of God Himself. We are being changed, and when the time comes for us to enter into the full presence of God at the return of Jesus, then we *shall* be changed (see 1 Cor. 15:52). But the process begins now, as we want to be like Jesus.

Victory!

10

Obstinate horses

We were staying at the famous Kantishna Roadhouse at the end of the road through Denali National Park. The scenic beauty of Polychrome Pass had amazed us, arctic foxes playing at their den had entranced us, and the close approach of a grizzly had thrilled us.

Now as we ate supper, reflecting on this glorious day, we were asked if we'd like to take a horse-and-cart ride out to Wonder Lake.

As evening fell, we huddled up in blankets at the back of the wagon. Even though it was late August, snow had fallen in the afternoon, and the scene was more like Christmas than a summer vacation!

The two-horse team trotted slowly up the hill out of the old mining settlement. Somehow they seemed reluctant to be out in the snow, and didn't make good time. As we crested the hill, one of the horses decided that was enough. To make its point, the animal just fell over sideways and lay on the ground! This tipped the cart, and we all jumped out in a hurry.

Marvin, our leader, got down and began arguing with the reluctant horse. "C'mon, boy, let's get movin'. Can't stay lyin' down here. Up you get. I said, *get up*. Don't be so foolish. I want you up on your feet right now!"

But the old horse wasn't having any of it. Resting, it didn't have any intention of moving for anybody. So then Marvin started in with his whip, but with no result. Some of the women began to get upset, sure he was tormenting a poor horse about to die. Marvin reassured them that this was just one of the horse's tricks. But no matter what Marvin did, he couldn't get the horse up. In the end he gave up, and we rode back in a van.

Next morning we all worried about the horse. The staff laughed at our concern, and said that the horse was fine and that it had won another victory over the tourists! One of the stable hands had gone up the hill and with some quiet words had the horse back on its feet, ready to walk home.

It made me think of the way we are too. Of how we are so often defeated—even by ourselves. We want to go in the right direction, we want to head toward the kingdom, but too often we fall down on the job. Our reluctant selves let us down, frustrating us and making us appear foolish. Bad habits, sinful desires, and imperfect strength overwhelm us. Are we like obstinate horses? So what should we do? Argue with ourselves, whip ourselves into shape? Is that how to win the victory? How much success did Marvin have with that kind of approach?

Winning the victory

How do we win spiritual victory? Is it through force of arms or strength of will? Is it by might and power? Or is it through God's gentle Spirit, who changes us from rebellious and reluctant horses dragging along duty's way to children running up the hill, eager to see their heavenly Father?

John tells us that we achieve victory through our faith. That may sound as if it really were something we do in our own strength. As if we were saying, "If I have enough of that magic ingredient— faith—then I can be victorious."

But think again. What exactly is this faith? Is it a special substance we can possess? No, faith is simply trusting in God. Now, without that trust we cannot have success, but the power and the strength come solely from God. Trust, by its very definition, means looking to someone else for help! Only as we turn to God can we succeed. In the words of William A. Ward: "God wants us to be victors, not victims; to grow, not grovel; to soar, not sink; to overcome, not to be overwhelmed."

Our trust is essential—for without it God cannot help us. But don't be fooled into thinking you have to gain it in your own strength. We need more faith—but that just means trusting God more! So the more we rely on God, the less we depend on ourselves and the more sure is the victory. "The first step on the way to victory is to recognize the enemy" (Corrie ten Boom). And who is the enemy? Is it primarily the devil, or is it the temptation of self-reliance?

John makes the essential requirement of trust very plain: "Who can defeat the world? Only the person who believes that Jesus is the Son of God" (1 John 5:5, TEV). Obviously, this means more than mental belief that the statement is true. As is frequently observed, even the devils believe—and tremble. But theirs is not a saving, transforming belief. Trust (faith) is belief in action, a definite reaching out in confidence to the only One who can save.

The basis of victory is then to be fully committed to the Victor! "Whoever has the Son has this life; whoever does not have the Son of God does not have life" (verse 12, TEV). John's repeated term is to "live in" or "abide." It is the essence of the Christian life. If we do not "live in union" with God, then we cannot truly live at all.

In union with God

We live in union with God by holding on to the message we have heard from the beginning (1 John 2:24), by living like Jesus (verses 5, 6), and by obeying the Spirit's teaching (verse 27). If we live in union with God, then, in turn, God lives in union with us (1 John 3:24; 4:16), and the Word of God lives in us (1 John 2:14).

Such ideas remind us of what Jesus said in His prayer recorded by John (see John 17:21-26). Jesus prays that His disciples may be one just as He and the Father are one. God wants to be so intimate with us that the only way He can express it is by the concept of being "in" each of us and we being in Him! We find our life, our hope, and our victory only as we are *in* God.

So what of this *in?* It is being *in* harmony with, *in* agreement with, *in* total acceptance of God's way as being absolutely right. Reconciled, harmonized, reunited—that's what God is speaking of and what He's trying to achieve.

Jesus the overcomer

The essential point is that we are on the winning side. We are not fighting some lonely battle by ourselves. Because we are on God's side, we can identify with all those who fight together with

Him. Should we doubt the outcome, Jesus has already proclaimed His ultimate and all-encompassing victory: "Take heart! I have overcome the world" (John 16:33).

We *should* doubt ourselves and our own powers, since the key is not in us, but in the One who has already overcome. Christ is the victor!

Have you noticed the many books that claim to be able to give you help in mastering a particular subject? *Brain Surgery Made Easy,* or *How to Build a Space Station,* or *101 Simple Steps to Intergalactic Travel,* or whatever! Such self-help books appeal to our desire for a "do-it-yourself" approach. But when it comes to our spiritual lives, such ideas can be disastrous.

I was reading a devotional book that tried to give helpful suggestions about how to fight temptation. I suppose they were ideas most of us might agree with. But the more I thought of how the author presented them, the more difficulties I noticed.

First suggestion: "You must pray about it." Good advice, but sometimes not so easy. After all, if you are really being tempted, you may not particularly *feel* like praying, or you may forget to do it anyway. As a surefire recipe for self-control, prayer can even be seen as a means by which *we* win the battle. Perhaps we believe that reciting a prayer is some magic charm against temptation. If prayer is just a method for control, then this too can be a kind of salvation by works, as we end up thinking we won the battle ourselves.

Second idea: "Don't think about your temptation." Have you ever deliberately tried not to think about the thing you're thinking about? In fact, the more you become concerned about a certain temptation, the more you end up dwelling on it. Try this for a moment. *Whatever you do, don't think about anything red for two minutes.* Well, did you? No, of course not. As soon as I mentioned the word "red," you were seeing red! You can reshape your thoughts, but not by making your temptation the point of what you're *not* thinking about.

Third recommendation: "Just do what you can, and God will do the rest." A kind of subsidized religious experience is suggested here. Maybe you manage 10 or 20 or 30 percent. Then God makes it up to 100 percent. I even remember a theology lecturer drawing such a graph to illustrate the point. God waits for you to do what you can on your own, and then He kicks in with His contribution when you give up. Again this makes us reliant on ourselves to some degree, and I suppose the suggestion is that the more we can accomplish on our own, the better. But it is not biblical!

Fourth suggestion: "You must try harder." Yes, we all know that. But what happens when you keep on trying and failing? Either you give up and walk away from it all, convinced you can never succeed, or you become shortsighted and don't see your sins anymore. As one pastor reminded me the other day: "The best thing about banging your head against a brick wall is when you stop!"

Lurking in all of these suggestions is the danger of self-reliance. Yes, we must want to change. Yes, we must accept God's healing salvation. Yes, we must do all we can to make sure we choose good over evil. But eventually the question of ability, power, and success is with God, not with us. Otherwise, we are appealing to our own willpower and determination, not the indwelling, converting power of Christ.

Let us leave the how-to ideas to the nonsalvational areas of our lives. The message of Scripture is that we cannot help ourselves. Only God can save us from our sinful selves. "In all these things we are more than conquerors through him who loved us" (Rom. 8:37). How are we conquerors? Not in our own strength, but *through Him who loved us*. That's where the source of victory lies.

"You, dear children, are from God and have overcome them, because the one who is in you is greater than the one who is in the world" (1 John 4:4). How do we overcome? By what we are? By the spiritual power we have generated? No, *because the One who is in you is greater*.

"But thanks be to God! He gives us the victory through our Lord Jesus Christ" (1 Cor. 15:57). How does victory come? Not by our ability and power. And by whom does it come? *Through our Lord Jesus Christ*.

For otherwise, what does it mean when we read "I have been crucified with Christ and I no longer live, but Christ lives in me" (Gal. 2:20)?

Again and again this is the message of the Bible. So why do we want to turn our salvation into a do-it-yourself project? Our victory results from our desire to maintain contact with God, to ensure that our relationship with Him is such that *He* can truly win the battles for us.

In all aspects of victory over temptation, go to God and "do not be overcome by evil, but overcome evil with good" (Rom. 12:21). We do not remove evil by concentrating on it. Rather, we crowd it out by focusing on the good.

Remember God's word to His people in olden times: "For the Lord your God is the one who goes with you to fight for you against your enemies to give you victory" (Deut. 20:4).

In those seemingly rare times when Israel looked back and saw that they were not responsible for their successes, then they could give praise where it was due: "It was not by their sword that they won the land, nor did their arm bring them victory; it was your right hand, your arm, and the light of your face, for you loved them" (Ps. 44:3).

The ultimate assurance is that "he who overcomes will inherit all this, and I will be his God and he will be my son" (Rev. 21:7). And remember that we can be overcomers only if God is our God first!

Christ's baptism began His specific ministry, and so He came "by water." He also showed through this symbol the way God operates. Although Christ did not need to be baptized as a symbol of repentance from sin, He still went ahead "to fulfill all righteousness" (Matt. 3:15). As a demonstration of God in human form, Jesus reveals His graciousness and His identification with us. Some among John's readers denied that God was present in Jesus on the cross. They suggested that divinity came upon Jesus at His baptism and then left before His death. So John writes:

"Jesus Christ is the one who came with the water of his baptism and the blood of his death. He came not only with the water, but with both the water and the blood" (1 John 5:6, TEV).

Through His baptism, Jesus shows us the way, and reveals God's salvation to us. But not only that. He did not just come to *show* us salvation, but to *be* our salvation. Christ was not only example, but Saviour! So to limit Christ to the events of His ministry after baptism "by water" and to exclude His death and resurrection is to miss the whole point. He also came "by blood"—and on the cross we truly see Christ as God. To deny that Christ was on the cross, and only the man Jesus, is the heresy that John is so emphatically condemning. For if we do not see God in Christ on the cross, then we cannot recognize the meaning of salvation, the truth about God, the evidence that sin kills, the lies of the devil—and all the rest of the answers that the cross provides to all the issues of the great controversy.

So what are the three witnesses that John describes (see 1 John 5:7, 8)?

The Spirit testifies of God in Christ: "But the Counsellor, the Holy Spirit, whom the Father will send in my name, will teach you all things and will remind you of everything I have said to you" (John 14:26).

The water testifies of God in Christ: "Jesus was baptized too. . . . And a voice came from heaven: 'You are my Son, whom I love; with you I am well pleased'" (Luke 3:21, 22).

The blood testifies of God in Christ: "For God was pleased to have all his fullness dwell in him, and through him to reconcile to himself all things . . . by making peace through his blood, shed on the cross" (Col. 1:19).

As a consequence, "God has given us eternal life, and this life has its source in his Son. Whoever has the Son has this life; whoever does not have the Son of God does not have life" (1 John 5:11, 12, TEV). It really is as simple as that!

Total Confidence

11

Confidence?

Tired but happy, we boarded the little fishing boat for our trip home. We had been out bird-watching all day on the Shetland is-land of Hascosay. Now back on the larger island of Unst, we were heading back to our base on Yell.

The swell was moderate, but somehow comforting as we headed south. Lulled by the rocking of the boat, I fell asleep with dreams of the day to come.

Suddenly I awoke with the boat still rocking, but without the comforting *putt-putt* of the diesel engine. "What's going on?" I asked anxiously.

"Dunno. Engine's quit," came the comforting reply.

I went over to take a look. Our skipper, first mate, deckhand, and mechanic was there by himself, up to the elbows in engine oil.

"What seems to be the problem?"

"Busted." Without looking up, he got on with the job.

I felt like screaming. My confidence was totally shattered. Here we were, drifting aimlessly on the high seas in some of the most treacherous waters off the Scottish coast. Shoals, reefs, jagged rocks—we'd seen them all. Now we were helpless, and at any mo-ment I thought I'd hear the smashing of timber on rock and the cry "Abandon ship!" How could he take it so lightly?

"Um, ever happen before?" My nervousness was showing, I was sure.

"Och, yes. This beast is temperamental, that's for sure."

"Where are we?" I felt foolish asking, but if we were about to be shipwrecked, I wanted to know.

"Well, we'd be 'bout three miles off Deadmen's Rocks."

Argh! Deadmen's Rocks. We were all going to drown. I could feel the panic rising. Which way were we drifting? Toward those rocks, for certain.

"Shouldn't we radio for help?"

He stopped and looked up at me. "And how would we do that without a radio?"

The reality of the situation overwhelmed me. Drifting, lost at sea, with no radio or radar. We were doomed! I sat down, making out my last will and testament in my head.

Moments later the reluctant engine chugged into life again, and we were on our way. Suddenly the whole scene changed. Confidence returned like a rush of adrenaline.

No longer was the sea full of menacing death, but alive with sparkling spray. No longer was the night brooding and oppressive, but open and full of shining stars. No longer was I anticipating my end. I was reborn.

Our circumstances and beliefs change our very lives. With God, whatever the situation, we have eternal hope. Without Him we have only the dark sea of everlasting death. It is God who transforms us and changes who we are into what we can be—with Him. God alone is our confidence. As we cruised home in a sheet of white spray, I dreamed of sailing home to God.

Despair and confidence

So many in the world today drift on a vast ocean of despair—lost, alone, without any hope, without any confidence that life will even continue, let alone that it will be good.

But John's words to his readers should inspire us, too: "We have confidence before God and receive from him anything we ask, because we obey his commands and do what pleases him" (1 John 3:21, 22). "Continue in him, so that when he appears we may be confident and unashamed before him at his coming" (1 John 2:28). "This is the confidence we have in approaching God: that if we ask anything according to his will, he hears us. And if we know that he hears us—whatever we ask—we know that we have what we asked of him" (1 John 5:14, 15).

John points to the reasons for being confident in God. We, of course, cannot expect to experience total trust in Him if we refuse to follow Him and His righteous commands (which, as we have seen before, are not really commands, but rather the outworking of true love and respect for God). If this is so, then our prayers will fall into line with God's plans and purposes. We need to continue in Him, so that as we ask in accordance with His will, He will give us anything we ask!

The key to prayer

The key to understanding prayer is to see it as a *communication* with God as our friend, and then to talk to Him, not just about our particular needs, but about all aspects of life. It is in this sense that we are to "pray without ceasing"—maintaining that link with God always.

Prayer is for *us*, and most of all, so we can "receive God"—to put into practice in our daily lives all His principles and aims.

Too often we pray for what *we* want, not what *God* wants. And so while God does *always* hear us, He does not always respond exactly as we expect. Yet this is also something to thank God for.

We must not neglect to pray. Even though God knows all our needs, even though He is aware of all our situations, even though we cannot tell Him anything He doesn't already know—He still wants us to express ourselves in our own way to Him. For prayer is truly not for God, but for us!

Often we pray for safety and protection. But is it always guaranteed? I ask this question because some church friends of mine died recently in a car crash. Another member tried to make sense of this by saying, "They probably forgot to ask for God's protection before they left." Is God this fickle? Does He allow things to happen just because of such a simple "mistake"?

We can refer to many promises God has made to take care of His children. But no promise totally guarantees this. The religious leaders in Jesus' time made this kind of mistake—seeing prosperity as a gift of God, while suffering and poverty were God's punishments. I know of too many good Christians who have suffered painful deaths, or experienced family tragedies, or seen their lives wrecked, to believe in a universal blanket of protection. What we *can* say is that if we should walk the rugged pathways, then God is still there. And remember that we are *safe in the Lord* (see 1 John 5:18) and that this life is only temporary. God prepares for us life in a city that He alone has made (see Heb. 11:10).

Even when we are angry, we should still pray. God never rejects those who speak with Him, even though they may not always pray in the most appropriate way. Perhaps the best prayers are those that come from the honest heart—such as the publican's prayer: "God, be merciful to me a sinner."

Nor should the idea that we are too sinful to come to God prevent us from praying. It is one of the devil's best weapons as he makes us feel too unworthy to even speak to our loving heavenly Father.

I have had too many members approach me as their pastor, believing they have committed the unpardonable sin. However, the fact that they feel such conviction of wrong at all and are so concerned shows that the Holy Spirit is still working on their hearts. The danger is not a sin that God refuses to forgive, but in the sin we choose not to ask forgiveness for. We need to pray together and bear one another's burdens (see Gal. 6:2).

That's why John advises: "If anyone sees his brother commit a sin that does not lead to death, he should pray and God will give him life" (1 John 5:16).

When God eventually gives up on those who refuse His offer of grace and mercy and allows them to go their own way, it is because they have become so inured to the pleadings of the Spirit that they have forever rejected them. For everyone there comes a time when probation closes—when God can declare their destiny chosen for all eternity. This is the "sin that leads to death" that John refers to (verse 16).

The final death of the wicked is the result of their own choice. Sin ends inevitably in this disastrous destination if we continually choose this route. If we finally and conclusively reject God, then He can do nothing more for us.

But John is quick to counter the idea that all sin leads relentlessly to death. Remembering God's "antidote" to sin, John writes that "there is a sin that does not lead to death" (verse 17). Considering what he has already written (see 1 John 2:1, 2; 3:5), it's clear that this kind of sin is the sin that has been repented of and been forgiven. Thus we cannot use the passage to excuse sin in our lives, assuming that our particular sin is one that does not lead to death!

The truth is that "we know that anyone born of God does not continue to sin" (1 John 5:18). So can we be assured of salvation only by making ourselves good? *Do you have to be good first before you can go to God?*

Although we say no, we often think so. We tell our children: "If you're good, you'll go to heaven." "If you're good, God will help you." "If you're good, God will love you." Which means that if we're *not* good, then God doesn't help us and He doesn't love us and He won't save us. Right? Dangerous reasoning!

How many times have I heard people say "God can't love me after what I've done," or "I'm not worthy of God's attention," or "How can I go to God when I'm like this?" So we put up barriers between us and God, and say to ourselves, "I can go to God only when I'm good."

But we have it all wrong. What did Jesus say?

"It is not the healthy who need a doctor, but the sick. I have not come to call the righteous, but sinners to repentance" (Luke 5:31, 32). Jesus was interested in those who considered themselves sinners, because those who regarded themselves as righteous wouldn't respond to His call to repent. As He said, only sick people go to see the doctor. Healthy people have no need of a physician.

And maybe Jesus meant more than that. Looking at the self-righteous Pharisees as He spoke, He saw the wickedness in their hearts and shook His head. After all, until we realize that we are *all* bad, how can God help? Those who think themselves well, Jesus said, will never go to the doctor—even though they may be in desperate need.

How many times have you heard stories of people who thought they were perfectly fit and healthy, and then suddenly died? They did not know their need. And often, if they had gone to the doctor, their illness could have been treated. Does that say something to you about how we should seek God? *Our confidence cannot be in ourselves, but only in God.*

A man came to Jesus and asked, "Teacher, what good thing must I do to get eternal life?" Jesus replied: "Why do you ask me about what is good? . . . There is only One who is good" (Matt. 19:16, 17).

The "rich young ruler," as we call him, had already shown his misunderstanding through his question. He thought you had to be good first.

The young man assumed that Jesus' message was the same as the common belief of his time—that God can work only with good people. He was looking to make himself right with God first by being good.

So Jesus made him think. The man had called Jesus "Teacher." Obviously he saw Jesus in a special way and recognized His evident goodness. But Jesus desired no compliments. Rather, He wanted the young man to see that all are bad. Only if he admitted that Jesus is divine could he call Him good, for, said Jesus, only God is good.

Quite a point: either you say that I'm God, or you're mistaken. Either you say that no one is good, or you're mistaken. Jesus throws a wrench in the works of every "good" person's thinking. Jesus' following words indicate His basic premise: nobody's good, and you can't get to God by being good first anyway.

In the end, when Jesus asked the young man to give up all his possessions, he still misunderstood. He thought Jesus wanted him to sell everything so that he might be considered good. No, Jesus wanted him to get rid of what he owned so that nothing would be in the way of God making him good.

He needed to see himself in the same state as tax gatherers and thieves and all the other low people of society. He was the same as they before God, and had just the same need. But his money and position prevented him from going to God as he should—a sinner needing salvation. He would approach Jesus only as a good man making a bargain with God: "I'm good, I keep the law, so reward me!"

Sadly, many of us do the same. We say, "God, look at me. Look at all I do for You. I'm good, rich, and have need of nothing." And God says, "Don't you know that you're poor and blind and naked?" (see Rev. 3:17). That is how we all stand before God—whether we think ourselves good or not. "All our righteousnesses are as filthy rags" (Isa. 64:6, KJV).

So Jesus says to you, as He did to that young man, "You're not good. Only One is good. Only God is good." We cannot make ourselves good. So we can only go to God as we are. Ignoring our so-called goodness, He accepts us just as we are—"warts and all!"

And then He begins the process of change. So don't let the evil one fool you. Nothing you have done can keep you from going to God. Nor can you ever say, "I'm not good enough." God doesn't want your goodness. He wants to *make* you good!

For that is the gospel—quite literally, the *good* news. The *good* news that Jesus came and died for you. The *good* news that He offers His love and salvation to you. The *good* news that He can do something for you—He can make you *good*.

We deceive ourselves when we look to our own good works and regard them as justifying ourselves before God. Or when we see our sinfulness and believe we cannot come to God. The truth is that "anyone who does what is good is from God" (3 John 11).

So our only safety is in being humble friends of God. Surely we could never improve upon John's conclusion: "We know that we are children of God, and that the whole world is under the control of the evil one. We know also that the Son of God has come and has given us understanding, so that we may know him who is true. And we are in him who is true—even in his Son Jesus Christ. He is the true God and eternal life" (1 John 5:19, 20). May we be confident in Him!

Don't Lose Out!

12

Children, our Father, and being lost

I sit and watch my children. Laughing, shouting, giggling, they play in the garden, splash in the paddling pool, whiz down the slide, soar high on the swing. Without a care in the world, they live their little lives to the full, busy until bedtime.

So what of me, the one they call Daddy? As their father I watch over them. I take care of the cuts and bruises that come as part of life, and, yes, deal with the odd argument that flares up between them. I feed them, care for them, protect them—all this and more, for I look and see lives just beginning. Here are individuals who need to learn as they grow, for they will not always be children. Children have the opportunity to play, to experiment, to be childish even. We don't expect total maturity in children. So my role is to give them the freedom they need, and yet also direct them in the way they should go, helping them to make the right decisions.

Father is the image God uses for the relationship between us and Him. We are His children, and as a loving Father He cares for and watches over us. But He knows we will not be immature forever. We too are growing and need to learn for ourselves. While there is always that relationship of being someone's child (and we are always God's children—for all eternity), still in this life we are growing and preparing for an adulthood in heaven.

This is why being called God's children is so wonderful!

God leads us, teaches us to walk, and takes us in His arms. He is the one whom we look up to, who shows us what is best, who wants to save and heal us from our sin sickness. Our Lord pleads with us to come to Him, and even if we should refuse and break His heart, He does not abandon us.

"When Israel was a child, I loved him and called him out of Egypt as my son. But the more I called to him, the more he turned away from me. . . . I was the one who taught Israel to walk. I took my people up in my arms, but they did not acknowledge that I took care of them. I drew them to me with affection and love. I picked them up and held them to my cheek; I bent down to them and fed them. . . . How can I give you up, Israel? How can I abandon you? . . . My heart will not let me do it! My love for you is too strong. I will not punish you in my anger; I will not destroy Israel again. For I am God and not man. I, the Holy One, am with you. I will not come to you in anger" (Hosea 11:1-9, TEV).

These are powerful, moving, emotional words from our loving Father, who only wants what is for our good. Yet time and again we turn away as rebellious children, rejecting all He longs to offer us.

Yet He still calls out to us, as a Father seeking His lost children.

Anyone who has "misplaced" a child knows the agony and heartache that immediately hits. My son Paul was on a shopping trip with us when he was small—just a toddler. In a clothing store we spent some time working out just what we could and could not afford. Then, turning around to leave, we found Paul had disappeared. It was as if he had vanished into thin air.

We started searching around, trying not to be too obvious at first. But then panic began to take over, and we moved faster, calling out, "Paul, Paul!"

Nothing.

I ran to the door and glanced down the street.

Nothing.

The sales assistants started looking. What did he look like? What was he wearing? Had he ever done this before? I began to feel like an unfit father. Ana was really upset by now, desperately anxious.

Trying to remain calm, I searched the whole floor area again. Of course, I was praying like mad. Returning to our original location, I tried to think. What would he have done? Where would he have gone?

After all, normally he was obedient and had never run off before.

As I stood there, emotionally drained, a little face peeked out from one of the clothing rails and said, "OK, Daddy. Found me."

Paul had decided we were playing hide-and-seek! He had no idea of all the pain and anguish he'd caused, or that we were about to call the police. The hugs and kisses that he received rather overwhelmed him, for he had only been playing a game!

Any spiritual lessons here?

1. We don't know the dangers that surround us, spiritually speaking.
2. We may not even know we're lost.
3. For some of us, we're just playing a game.
4. Our Father is just as eager for us to respond to His call.
5. We pray about what we really care about.
6. Only when we realize our situation can God save us.
7. The whole of heaven is out looking for us, wanting to save the lost.
8. God overlooks our foolishness and willingly welcomes us back.

And so on—think of others for yourself.

Family

The atmosphere and language of 2 John is that of family. Even the church John is writing to he identifies as "the chosen lady and her children" (2 John 1). The apostle identifies God as Father, Jesus as Son. And John remarks, "How happy I was to find that some of your children live in the truth, just as the Father commanded us" (2 John 4, TEV).

This reminds us of that continuing theme of "children of God" that runs through John's previous letter. And his concern in writing this brief letter is similar to that of 1 John. He wants to make sure that deceitful impostors (see 2 John 7) do not lead any of God's children astray. Most of all, John is concerned that no one loses out in salvation.

Too many people are convinced that life is "out to get them," that they "never have any luck," that "the world is against them." If you have a tendency to think this way, read 2 John again and understand that God does not want you to lose out.

So don't throw salvation away—not now, not ever!

Throwing it all away

I think of Mark, who chose to go to a state university rather than Bible college, and within months had completely lost his faith. It was not surprising, since the lecturers were telling him the Bible was full of contradictions and was irrelevant for the modern world.

I think of John, who had grown up in a Christian home and yet threw it all away for what he saw as a successful career. One great opportunity led to another, until he had made a real fortune. But as quickly as he made it, he lost it, and the last I heard he was living in a one-room apartment with a woman who was not his wife. Tragic. And even if he had kept all his money, I would still feel he had thrown it all away, since the richer he became, the less time he had for God or the church. In the end he just gave up coming, and when we called him, he told us he was too busy.

I think of Amy, who seemed to have it all—happiness, looks, intelligence. She had grown up knowing and loving the God of our salvation. But when she hit her teens, all her happiness evaporated as she started experimenting with sex and drugs and all the rest. Before she had even lived, she was dead. She threw it all away by taking her own life.

Throwing it all away. So easy to do, especially since that's what the devil wants. "Go on; God doesn't care," he tells us. "Give up; don't bother trying. The best way to get rid of temptation is to give in to it," he whispers in our ears.

But you and I know that only as we continue and don't give up can we be truly happy in the arms of our loving Lord.

Jesus: both God and man

John reminds us that love means walking in obedience to God's commands (see 2 John 6). Again and again he emphasizes that obedience springs naturally from agreement with, admiration of, and respect for God, the one who is naturally right and righteous.

As John defines it, losing out on one's salvation results from following the deceivers. Who are these particular deceivers? Those "who do not acknowledge Jesus Christ as coming in the flesh" (2 John 7). Some men and women of John's time believed that the body was evil and that God could not have come in the flesh, as Jesus claimed. He either only "appeared" to dwell on earth, or, they suggested, divinity came upon an earthly Jesus at His baptism and then left before His death on the cross. But how can we apply this today? Who are those who deny the humanity of Jesus today?

Many beliefs and practices undercut the reality of Jesus Christ. Some say He never really existed as a historical person. Others disagree with His recorded message and mission. Perhaps the debates and disputes over the nature of Christ can come right down to this: Can we really accept both the divinity and the humanity in one nature—the unique Jesus?

Ask people today what they think of Jesus, and you get many answers: "He was a great teacher." "He was a good man." "He was a prophet of God." And so on. But all such responses are like those from the deceivers John mentions. They all reject the reality of Jesus Christ as the Son of God in human form. So let us avoid such speculation and rejection of God's truth, and make sure that we're not led astray and that we don't throw away all we once stood for.

For as John continues: "Anyone who runs ahead and does not continue in the teaching of Christ does not have God; whoever continues in the teaching has both the Father and the Son" (2 John 9). We must avoid the temptation to speculate and conjecture and theorize lest we "run ahead" of God and His truth.

I went out with a church group for a hike through a forest. The kids ran on ahead, enjoying the summer day out in the countryside. But even though they thought they knew the way, by running on ahead they led themselves astray. They took a wrong turn and wandered off in a different direction. It required much searching on our part to bring them back to the right way!

We all need to stay together as the family of God, and most of all remain together with God. Otherwise, it's not just the missing one who loses out—in a sense we all lose out if anyone is lost. God summons each of us to run the race, to help each other, and to keep our eyes on the prize—the prize of being one with God, now and forever.

Running the race

I remember watching a marathon race. The front-runner had given his all when he stumbled into the final lap around the stadium. The crowd cheered him on as he struggled to continue. But just yards from the finish line his legs crumpled and he collapsed in sight of the prize. We all felt the tragedy.

Paul speaks about the need to strain toward the finishing tape: "I press on toward the goal to win the prize for which God has called me heavenward in Christ Jesus" (Phil. 3:14). And he also warns about letting anything distract us: "Do not let anyone who delights in false humility and the worship of angels disqualify you for the prize. Such a person goes into great detail about what he has seen, and his unspiritual mind puffs him up with idle notions" (Col. 2:18).

Using the same imagery again, Paul elsewhere explains that we have to train and prepare and really run the race (see 1 Cor. 9:24-27). How foolish, after having done so much, to lose out. Or to use another of Paul's images: after having done so much for others, wouldn't it be foolish to become a castaway (verse 27)?

We need to truly think of where we're going and why. To focus on the reward is not to be selfish. Of course, if we're too busy thinking about the streets of gold and all the jewels, then we surely have our priorities wrong. But the Christian's reward is worth thinking about, in the same way as a prisoner held underground strains toward the light. See what Jesus and the New Testament say about the reward of those who love God:

The greatest reward

"Rejoice and be glad, because great is your reward in heaven" (Matt. 5:12).

"For the Son of Man is going to come in his Father's glory with his angels, and then he will reward each person according to what he has done" (Matt. 16:27).

"But love your enemies, do good to them, and lend to them without expecting to get anything back. Then your reward will be great, and you will be sons of the Most High, because he is kind to the ungrateful and wicked" (Luke 6:35).

"What then is my reward? Just this: that in preaching the gospel I may offer it free of charge, and so not make use of my rights in preaching it" (1 Cor. 9:18).

"You know that you will receive an inheritance from the Lord as a reward. It is the Lord Christ you are serving" (Col. 3:24).

"[Moses] regarded disgrace for the sake of Christ as of greater value than the treasures of Egypt, because he was looking ahead to his reward" (Heb. 11:26).

"Behold, I am coming soon! My reward is with me, and I will give to everyone according to what he has done" (Rev. 22:12).

But for me the greatest reward, and the best reason for not giving up or losing out or throwing it all away, is that I shall be forever with God my friend. As John looks forward to meeting his friends, so do I: "I hope to visit you and talk with you face to face, so that our joy may be complete" (2 John 12). Face-to-face with my loving Lord—what an incredible day that will be.

"Now the dwelling of God is with men, and he will live with them. They will be his people, and God himself will be with them and be their God" (Rev. 21:3). May we all choose to be there!

Imitating Good

13

Why John?

Having enjoyed so much of John's writings, I asked myself why he is so appealing, so admirable. My conclusion was that he is the disciple who most closely resembles Jesus. Even his thoughts seem to have become similar to Christ's. If you compare John's writings with the words of Jesus, you find that they parallel each other. In many ways John allowed the truth to change him so completely that instead of being a "son of thunder" he became a true brother of Jesus Christ.

By beholding we become changed (see 2 Cor. 3:18). As we see the wonderful transformation in John's life we begin to understand what God can do for us. It is not enough to *say* that we believe in Jesus; we have to *show* a Christlike spirit in our personal lives. This forms the basis of John's appeal in his last brief letter.

The truth is that we become like those we respect, value, and admire. In our world today, who are those we follow? Who are our role models, the persons we pattern our lives after? Media figures? Pop "idols" (even using the word tells us about "worship" straight-away!)? Movie "stars" (who shine with almost divine brightness in the eyes of their fans)? Characters of the books we read? Political figures? Actors in our favorite TV programs?

Who are you patterning your life after? And what principles are you adopting? What behavior patterns are you forming? For we are being changed, for good or bad, every moment. As Paul pleads: "Don't let the world around you squeeze you into its own mould, but let God re-make you so that your whole attitude of mind is changed" (Rom. 12:2, Phillips).

Paul goes even further: "Therefore I urge you to imitate me" (1 Cor. 4:16). "You became imitators of us and of the Lord" (1 Thess. 1:6). "Remember your leaders, who spoke the word of God to you. Consider the outcome of their way of life and imitate their faith" (Heb. 13:7).

Whom to imitate

Even though it may seem rather vain to tell others to imitate you, this is the very way that we learn—from imitation. Copying the teacher is the heart of learning that leads to understanding. Only as we see *how* can we really say we *know*.

You can explain what to do with words, draw diagrams, build models, write textbooks, and paint pictures, but until you can help students actually do it, they can never truly learn. Imagine you're a car mechanic. You want to teach a class how to strip down an engine. What are you going to do? Refer them to the manual? Yes. Show them posters on the wall? Yes. But until you take that engine apart yourself and put the tools in the students' hands and demonstrate the right way to go about it, they will not *really* know how it is done. As Aesop said in his fable *"The Crab and Her Mother:* "Example is better than precept."

So too with our communication of God's truth. Only as we stop talking and painting pictures can we really begin. We have to live out the Christian life and say, *"This* is how it is!"

What about our spiritual life? Whom are we to imitate? There's nothing wrong in imitating the good lives of other Christians, as long as we realize that all of us can make mistakes. John's advice is not just to imitate others uncritically, but to copy what we have decided is good.

The imitation of God

Jesus Himself specifically identified the reason that He came to earth: "In fact, for this reason I was born, and for this I came into the world, to testify to the truth" (John 18:37).

Because from the beginning the devil has been "a liar and the father of lies" (John 8:44), Jesus came to demonstrate that what Satan said was a lie and what God said was the truth. There was no other way God could do it. The only way He could prove what He was really like was to come in person so everybody could see! Jesus' primary purpose in coming to our world was to demonstrate the truth about God. And if we are trying to make God known, we must first look to God in Jesus. "No one has ever seen God, but God the One and Only, who is at the Father's side, has made him known" (John 1:18).

How did Jesus reveal God? Think for a moment.

How He came—as a baby. Not with great wealth, power, or position, but as the child of some poor peasant in a far-off corner of the Roman Empire.

How He grew up—not with the benefit of an advanced education, not with a lot of personal possessions. Working hard to earn His food, He lived just like millions of other human beings.

How He began His ministry—by being baptized like us (even though He had no need to).

How He performed His first miracle—water into wine was a perfect demonstration of God's generosity.

How He healed thousands upon thousands—miracles that Jesus performed to show that God wants us to be well, physically and spiritually, and that He does not cause pain and suffering, disease and death. Above all, these gifts of healing, feeding, and caring demonstrate the love of God in a dramatic way.

How He spoke—not with great oratory, not bouncing up and down in a rage, but firmly and lovingly, showing people the truth and the way back to their loving Father. His parables (for example, the prodigal son welcomed home by his weeping, loving father) demonstrate God in a powerfully compelling way.

Jesus lived as God among us—Emmanuel. That's why Jesus said: "If you really knew me, you would know my Father as well. From now on, you do know him and have seen him" (John 14:7).

If you know Jesus, you know God. It's as simple as that. But poor Philip couldn't believe that, so he asked to see the Father (verse 8). How Jesus must have sighed as He explained to Philip: "Anyone who has seen me has seen the Father" (verse 9).

So what are we to do? How are we to speak well of God? What is to be our pattern for "imitation"? What is to be our main message?

What's the most important thing we have to say? The third

angel's message? The Second Coming? The Sabbath? The caring church?

No. *The heart of the message is the good news of and about God.* Let us look again at what we're saying. We're not trying to convince people about a system of creeds to which you agree. We're not trying to make people healthy so that they will join our organization. We're not trying to so scare and frighten people that they become part of the "remnant church." That's not God's way. His way is to show what He's really like. That must be our way, too. In speaking of the goodness of God we must reveal to others what God is truly like.

Above all, *"we do not preach ourselves, but Jesus Christ as Lord"* (2 Cor. 4:5). God, the Creator, has given us the light of His marvelous truth so that we will know Him as reflected in the life of Jesus: "God . . . made his light shine in our hearts to give us the light of the knowledge of the glory of God in the face of Christ" (verse 6). That's our message—*God.* And He reveals Himself through *you and me!*

The three examples

In his Third Epistle the apostle presents three examples of believers in the church. Which example we choose to follow is up to us. But we must be under no illusions as to the different kinds of lives and their different results.

The passage we are examining reveals actual people and how they relate to one another in specific church situations. We wish we knew more, but from the brief notes we have, it's clear that nothing much has changed over the years! Human nature still needs to be transformed by the Spirit so that those who call themselves Christians will become more and more Christlike.

Even though we have very few details, the three persons mentioned give us an understanding of what John is dealing with and examples of the impact of their actions.

Gaius. John's commendation indicates that Gaius has chosen to live under the controlling influence of the truth. Truth has a compelling quality of rightness that is inescapable. You cannot fake the truth.

In his other writings John speaks much of the influence truth should have on us. Unless we are changed by what the truth means, then we are living a lie. For Gaius, this means that he has been faithful to his beliefs. All too often those who claim to be Christians demonstrate otherwise. The idea of "faithfulness" to the truth is most important—we need to stand firm and not allow anything to move us away from what we know to be true.

The apostle also praises Gaius for his actions. "My dear friend, you are so faithful in the work you do for your fellow Christians, even when they are strangers" (3 John 5, TEV). The church member has a positive, warm, and loving attitude—one that is certainly worth copying. To be known for such Christian hospitality is a real blessing, one that speaks more than words.

We have all been in the situation of being visitors to another church, and know how encouraging it is to be welcomed and made to feel at home. Such a loving attitude will be spoken of (3 John 6) as evidence of the truth behind what we believe.

Diotrephes. The opposite to Gaius is this man who has chosen to operate from anti-Christian principles. That may sound strong, but the truth is that anyone who misuses power and tells lies is following the ways of Satan, especially within the church, where such things should never happen.

So what exactly are the "charges" against Diotrephes? (See 3 John 9, 10.)

1. He has refused to accept the authority of church leaders, even rejecting John, the senior statesman of the church at the time, the only one left alive who was with Jesus as an apostle. While we must not tolerate an authoritarian leadership, it is right and proper to follow the counsel of God-given leaders.

2. He has misrepresented others and told lies. Again this is part of his power strategy, for in lying about John and his fellow workers Diotrephes can maintain his own position in the church. But to do such things within the church is to emulate the devil, who is the father of lies (see John 8:44) and who has continually misrepresented truth and smeared God's character. The seriousness of this offense is the fact that others will look at Diotrephes as a local leader in the church and believe that he truly represents Christianity. Most damaging of all is that the picture of God Diotrephes shows to the world is distorted and corrupted.

3. He has used his position of church power to prevent others from sharing Christian truth. In controlling who spoke to the church or even who visited the members, Diotrephes has made himself a self-appointed censor of truth. While even those who are acting from right principles will wish to make sure that all that is said and done in church is in harmony with what we believe, truth does not need our defense in a dictatorial way. To use force is always contrary to God's way of government.

4. Diotrephes has clearly demonstrated his misuse of church power and the exercise of force by trying to drive anyone who doesn't agree with him out of the church. To censure or disfellowship those who simply disagree with you is an unacceptable method of church government. Sadly, church discipline has been used in a similar way today as a method of retaliation. But that is not its true purpose. Church discipline exists to win erring members back to the truth, not to drive them away.

So John tries to help Gaius deal with the traumatic situation in his church. He encourages Gaius, shows where Diotrephes is wrong, and then calls on Gaius to imitate the good, not the bad.

Demetrius. John does not leave the situation as a showdown between Gaius and Diotrephes, however. He mentions Demetrius to Gaius, and speaks very well of him. It's almost as if John is saying, "Here's a fellow friend in the church who can support you." We all need friends in church, ones who can help us on our way. But we need to choose the good, those whom "truth itself speaks well of" (3 John 12, TEV). John backs this up with a personal recommendation of Demetrius, also mentioning that "everyone speaks well of Demetrius" (verse 12, TEV).

Wouldn't it be good to know a little more about Demetrius? Surely some more details would be interesting! And yet even in these few words we have all we need to know. For what better epitaph for a Christian than to be "well spoken of by everyone—and even by the truth itself" (3 John 12).

So John ends his letter. Maybe he pauses before he writes the last lines, considering his friends all around the various churches, and those in this congregation in particular. Perhaps he smiles to himself with happy memories, and, as when writing his Second Epistle, ends with the thought that he would have liked to write more, but that he hopes to be able to see them all soon. Then he will be able to speak with them face-to-face (3 John 13). Face-to-face—the way we want to speak with our friends. And one day we will speak face-to-face with God, our greatest friend.

Taking his pen for the last time, he writes his final words. Peace to you. Greetings to friends from friends here. I'm sure that these words meant much to Gaius. After being in a church with such controversy, to know there are friends thinking of you offers much comfort. But most of all, Gaius must wish for what John sends—peace!

So for all of us. Despite the problems, despite all the troubles of life, God is still there, and we shall be with Him and His friends forever and live in His wonderful peace.